MW01245235

Critical Thinking

2 Books in 1: The Fundamental and Concise Guide to Master Smart Decision Making, Intelligent Reasoning, Negotiating, Deep and Quick Analysis, and Independent Thinking Like Never Before

BY

Henry Fennimore

Critical Thinking

Critical Thinking

Critical Thinking

The Fundamental and Concise Guide to
Master Smart Decision Making,
Intelligent Reasoning, Negotiating, Deep
and Quick Analysis, and Independent
Thinking Like Never Before
Part-1

BY

Henry Fennimore

Table of Contents

Critical Thinking

The Fundamental and Concise Guide to
Master Smart Decision Making,
Intelligent Reasoning, Negotiating, Deep
and Quick Analysis, and Independent
Thinking Like Never Before
Part-2

BY

Henry Fennimore

Table of Contents

Critical Thinking

acknowledge that the author is not engaging in the rendering of legal, financial, medical or professional advice. The content within this book has been derived from various sources. Please consult a licensed professional before attempting any techniques outlined in this book.

By reading this document, the reader agrees that under no circumstances is the author responsible for any losses, direct or indirect, which are incurred as a result of the use of information contained within this document, including, but not limited to, — errors, omissions, or inaccuracies.

Description

One of a kind in context, this book gives a general way to deal with basic reasoning aptitudes that can be applied to all controls. With an accentuation on composing, just as on choosing what to accept or do, it offers broadened dialogs, models, and practice of such abilities as watching, making decisions, arranging investigations, and creating thoughts and choices.

Characterizes the structure and substance of the basic deduction course, at schools and colleges the nation over. This incorporates the ideas of basic intuition, with models significant to understudies.

Business associations are in consistent and quickening emergency. This reality is clear to such an extent that we quit monitoring it completely and we concentrate on specific regions rather, attempting to address them in segregation. Likewise, while tending to huge issues influencing business, we look for arrangements and - which is far more terrible point of view inside the business space itself: we go to directors, experts and scholastics spend significant time in different parts of business. This nearsighted mindset has discovered its way to the bigger space of financial aspects and governmental issues which are being run as organizations, further strengthening the overall emergency.

Our reason is straightforward: to take care of our issues or to trigger positive change we have to look outside of the business area, even outside of the cutting edge attitude that brought forth business in any case, go past transient speculations, reach back to the basics, draw on immortal shrewdness and discover approaches to apply them in the present setting.

While the book seeks after an interdisciplinary way to deal with basic reasoning, giving models and outlines from various subjects and fields of research, it likewise gives methodologies to assist perusers with distinguishing the strategies and benchmarks that are normal for basic intuition in their picked parts of learning, in their working environment, and in their own lives. The idea of a contention is reached out past its philosophical roots to incorporate experimentation, testing, estimation, approach advancement and evaluation, and stylish gratefulness as exercises that require basic reasoning. The legitimate, center ideas of basic reasoning are introduced in a thorough yet casual manner, with inventive and down to earth methodologies for characterizing, dissecting, and assessing reasons and contentions any place they are found.

Critical Thinking

CHAPTER 1

History

John Dewey (1910: seventy four, eighty two) brought the term 'significant addressing' as the name of a scholastic expectation, which he perceived with an efficient attitude of considerations. Extra ordinarily, he called the objective 'intelligent thought', 'intelligent reasoning', 'reflection', or basically 'thought' or 'thinking'. He depicts his book as composed for 2 capacities. The first was to help people to understand the family relationship of adolescents' neighborhood interest, ripe innovativeness and love of trial request to the therapeutic frame of mind. The subsequent one changed into to help individuals to remember how detecting this family relationship in instructional practice "could make for man or lady satisfaction and the decrease of social waste" (iii). He noticed that the considerations in the digital book got solidness in the Laboratory staff in Chicago.

Dewey's considerations have been put into training by means of some of the schools that took an interest inside the 8-year look at in the Nineteen Thirties sponsored by utilizing the cutting edge instruction connection in the America. For this examine, 300 schools consented to remember for affirmation alumni of 30 settled on auxiliary resources or school structures from over the U.S. A. who tried different things with the substance and strategies of instructing, regardless of whether the alumni had now not completed the then-recommended auxiliary school educational program. One reason for the examination changed into to discover through investigation and experimentation how auxiliary schools inside the usa should serve youths all the more accurately.each trial school transformed into free to trade the educational program as it saw coordinate, anyway the universities concurred that instructing procedures and the presence of the school need to follow the idea (recently supported by Dewey) that people grow by means of doing things which can be huge to them, and that the fundamental rationale of the optional school was to control youthful individuals to comprehend, acknowledge and remain the popularity based way of life highlight of the usa. Especially, school authorities accepted that youthful people in a majority rule government need to build up the dependancy of intelligent reasoning and ability in taking care of issues. undergrads' work inside the examination space therefore comprised extra as often as possible of an issue to be comprehended than an exercise to be educated. primarily in math and innovation, the resources tried giving understudies revel in clear, legitimate addressing as they tackled issues. The report of 1 trial workforce, the college school of Ohio state school, explained this point of upgrading understudies' pondering:

Imperative or intelligent addressing starts with the detecting of an issue. it is a high-caliber of idea working with the goal that you can clear up the issue and to accomplish a speculative end that is bolstered by all to be had records. it's far in actuality a strategy for issue fixing requiring the utilization of inventive discernment, highbrow genuineness, and sound judgment. it's far the premise of the strategy for clinical request. The satisfaction of vote based system depends to an enormous degree at the attitude and capacity of occupants to expect harshly and brilliantly roughly the difficulties which need to of need go up against them, and to improve the best of their scrutinizing is one of the fundamental fantasies about tutoring. (Commission on the Relation of staff and school of the advanced preparing association.

The 8-year watch had an evaluation staff, which created, in discussion with the schools, appraisals to degree components of understudy progress that fell outside the point of convergence of the customary educational program. The appraisal group of laborers named a great deal of the resources' said focuses under the ordinary heading "unwavering discernment" or "significant reasoning". To create checks of accomplishment of this immense objective, they recognized five covering parts of it: capacity to translate measurements, abilities related with an expertise of the character of proof, and the abilities to apply ideas of science, of social research and of consistent thinking. The 8-year watch moreover had a school gathering of laborers, coordinated by a board of trustees of college overseers, whose task changed into to decide how pleasantly the trial schools had arranged their alumni for school. The school work force as looked at the general execution of 1,475 undergrads from the trial resources with an indistinguishable wide assortment of graduates from conventional universities, coordinated two by two with the guide of intercourse, age, race, educational energy evaluations, home and system verifiable past, leisure activities, and potentially fate. They presumed that, on 18 proportions of understudy accomplishment, the alumni of the exploratory schools did a moderately higher procedure than the evaluation establishment. The alumni from the six generally regular of the trial schools affirmed no gigantic or relentless varieties. The alumni from the six most test resources, then again, had an extraordinary arrangement additional varieties in support of them. The alumni of the two greatest trial resources, the college group of laborers stated:

Outperformed their examination organizations with the guide of colossal edges in scholarly achievement, scholarly interest, therapeutic way to deal with inconveniences, and enthusiasm for present day undertakings. The distinctions of their pick have been considerably more prominent in standard cleverness, in diversion of dissecting, [in] investment in expressions of the human experience, in triumphing non-instructive distinctions, and in all elements of college presence with the exception of more then likely interest in sports exercises and social exercises. This sort of resources turned into an individual school with understudies from advantaged family units and the option the trial segment of an open staff with undergrads from non-favored families. The school group of laborers said that the alumni of the 2 schools had been undefined from each other regarding college accomplishment.

In 1933 Dewey gave an obviously revamped rendition of his How We accept , with the sub-name "A rehashing of the connection of intelligent addressing to the educative system". In spite of the way that the repetition keeps the essential structure and substance of the first digital book, Dewey made some of alterations. He revamped and streamlined his consistent examination of the strategy for reflected picture, made his considerations more clear and increasingly specific, changed the expressions 'enlistment' and 'conclusion' by methods for the expressions 'control of data and verification' and 'oversee of thinking and thoughts', brought more noteworthy representations, reworked sections, and reconsidered the parts on instructing to reflect alterations in schools since 1910. exceptionally, he questioned 1 -sided practices of a couple "exploratory" and "present day" resources that permitted youths opportunity anyway gave them no steerage, raising as shocking practices oddity and assortment for the good of their own one of a kind, stories and sports with genuine materials anyway of no instructional significance, regarding arbitrary and separated diversion just as it were a trial, inability to abridge web achievement on the quit of a request, non-educative activities, and cure of the coach as an immaterial angle in inclination to as "the highbrow chief of a social association". with out clarifying his reasons, Dewey disposed of the first version's utilizes of the expressions 'significant' and 'uncritical', therefore settling solidly on 'reflected picture' or 'intelligent reasoning' on the grounds that the ideal term for his test depend. inside the amended release, the word 'pivotal' happens best once, in which Dewey composes that "an individual may not be adequately indispensable about the thoughts that emerge to him" ; being critical is as an outcome an issue of reflection, no longer its total. In assessment, the 8-yr see by the progressive preparing affiliation managed 'crucial addressing' and 'intelligent intuition' as equivalent words.

inside a similar length, Dewey worked together on a records of the Laboratory school in Chicago with previous educators from the school . The records portrays the school's educational program and association, sports designed for developing abilties, mother and father' inclusion, and the direct of mind that the kids gained. A finishing up chapter 11 assesses the school's accomplishments, considering a triumph its arranging of the educational program to relate to the regular improvement of the developing infant. In two supplements, the creators depict the advancement of Dewey's ideas of instruction and Dewey himself portrays the possibility of the Chicago try .

Glaser (1941) audits in his doctoral paper the technique and aftereffects of a test in the improvement of significant addressing directed in the fall of 1938. He characterizes fundamental addressing as Dewey depicted intelligent pondering:

Basic reasoning requires an industrious endeavor to take a gander at any conviction or expected state of ability inside the gentle of the evidence that supports it and the likewise ends to which it tends. In the test, 8 exercise devices coordinated at improving significant addressing aptitudes were educated to four evaluation 12 unreasonable workforce classes, with pre-check and distribute check of the researchers the utilization of the Otis brief-Scoring scholarly capacity test and the Watson-Glaser appraisals of critical addressing (created as a team with Glaser's exposition support, Goodwin Watson). The normal advantage in scores on those checks become more noteworthy to a measurably decent estimated degree a portion of the understudies who get:

The part of basic pondering which appears to be greatest inclined to broad improvement is the outlook of being arranged to remember in a mindful way the issues and subjects that come inside the assortment of 1's revel in. An outlook of needing proof for standards is additional worry to stylish exchange. improvement of expertise in applying the strategies for consistent request and thinking, yet, is by all accounts specifically identified with, and in reality limited by methods for, the acquisition of relevant comprehension and certainties in regards to the difficulty or concern depend towards which the believing is to be coordinated.

Retest rankings and detectable conduct showed that understudies in the intercession association held their blast in capacity to expect altogether for at any rate a half year after the interesting direction. In 1948 an assortment of U.S. school analysts chose to expand scientific classifications of instructional exercise focuses with an ordinary jargon that they may use for talking with each other about investigate things. the first of those scientific classifications, for the subjective area, showed up in 1956 and included crucial addressing targets. It has come to be called Bloom's scientific classification. A subsequent scientific classification, for the full of feeling area, and a third scientific categorization, for the psychomotor space respected later. everything about scientific categorizations is various leveled, with accomplishment of a superior instructive goal claimed to require accomplishment of comparing decline scholarly destinations.

Blossom's scientific categorization has six fundamental classes. From most minimal to most elevated, they're data, understanding, programming, assessment, blend, and assessment. Inside each class, there are sub-classes, likewise sorted out progressively from the instructively preceding the instructively back. The base class, however called 'data', is restricted to destinations of recollecting records and having the option to remember or get it, absent a lot of change past sorting out it The five better classes are as one named "scholarly capabilities and capacities" The term is without a doubt some other call for significant pondering aptitudes and abilities:

Notwithstanding the way that data or comprehension is distinguished as an essential result of tutoring, not many educators could be fulfilled to regard this as the essential or the sole result of training. What is required is some proof that the researchers can do something with their skill, that will be, that they could pursue the measurements to new conditions and inconveniences. It is additionally foreseen that researchers will get summed up strategies for dealing with new inconveniences and new materials.

Therefore, it's miles expected that after the researcher experiences a shiny new issue or circumstance, he will pick the exact strategy for assaulting it and will bring to experience the significant records, every record and thoughts. This has been marked "basic pondering" by method for a few, "intelligent reasoning" through Dewey and others, and "critical thinking" by means of by and by others. In the scientific classification, we have utilized the expression "highbrow capacities and gifts".

Perception and sharpness objectives, as their names propose, include ability and utilizing information. Basic reasoning aptitudes and abilities show up inside the three most extreme classes of assessment, combination and assessment. The consolidated variant of Bloom's scientific categorization gives the resulting instances of destinations at those levels:

Assessment objectives: potential to comprehend implicit suspicions, potential to test the consistency of speculations with given records and presumptions, capacity to perceive the general techniques used in promoting, publicity and distinctive enticing substances

Union goals: arranging thoughts and proclamations recorded as a hard copy, potential to advocate methods for looking at a speculation, potential to detail and direct theories.

Assessment targets: capacity to recommend sensible paradoxes, complexity of head hypotheses about explicit societies.

The assessment, combination and appraisal focuses in Bloom's scientific classification all in all came to be known as the "better-request pondering abilities". In spite of the fact that the assessment combination appraisal assortment emulates arranges in Dewey's (1933) sensible examination of the intelligent reasoning procedure, it has not normally been embraced as a model of an essential pondering framework. Simultaneously as complimenting the helpful cost of its proportion of 5 classes of addressing objectives to in any event one classification of think about targets, Ennis (1981b) factors out that the sorts need criteria important all through subjects and area names. for instance, assessment in science is so not quite the same as investigation in writing that there isn't in every case bounty point in showing assessment as well known kind of reasoning. So also, the proposed pecking order seems faulty on the higher phases of Bloom's scientific classification. For instance, ability to recommend intelligent paradoxes barely shows up extra muddled than the capacity to compose proclamations and musings recorded as a hard copy.

A modified rendition of Bloom's scientific classification recognizes the alleged subjective framework in an instructive objective (comprehensive of being equipped for consider, to contrast or with test) from the objective's educational substance ("information"), which can be genuine, applied, procedural, or metacognitive. The outcome is a so-known as "Scientific categorization table" with 4 lines for the styles of educational substance material and six segments for the six chief types of subjective system. The creators call the kinds of subjective way through action words, to recommend their status as scholarly sports. They trade the call of the 'appreciation' class to 'perceive' and of the 'blend' classification to 'make', and switch the request for amalgamation and assessment.

The outcome is a posting of six most significant sorts of subjective strategy pointed toward with the guide of instructors: remember, secure, watch, look at, assess, and make. The creators keep the possibility of a chain of command of expanding unpredictability, however understood some cover, for instance among comprehension and applying. What's more, that they hold the idea that basic pondering and bother explaining diminish all through the additional complex intellectual techniques. The expressions 'basic pondering' and 'issue fixing', they compose:

Are comprehensively utilized and by and large will in general rise as touchstones of educational program accentuation. Each by and large comprise of a determination of exercises that is most likely sorted in different cells of the Taxonomy table. This is, in some random model, focuses on that include critical thinking and significant reasoning most extreme likely call for psychological strategies in a few classifications at the procedure measurement. As a case, to think seriously around a difficulty likely involves some Conceptual mastery to look into the trouble. At that point, you'll have the option to assess unmistakable perspectives as far as the criteria and, perhaps, Create an interesting, yet faultless frame of mind in this issue.

Inside the changed scientific categorization, just some sub-classes, for example, inducing, have enough shared trait to be treated as an awesome imperative reasoning capacity that would ponder and evaluated as an in vogue limit. A milestone commitment to philosophical grant at the idea of basic reasoning become a A proposed reason for contemplates in the educating and appraisal of significant addressing potential" Ennis took as his starting element a thought of essential pondering set forward with the guide of B. Othanel Smith:

We will thought in expressions of the tasks worried inside the test of proclamations which we, or others, may concur with. A speaker declares, for instance, that "Opportunity strategy that the decisions in the US's proficient exertion are made now not inside the brains of an administration anyway in the free commercial center". Presently in the event that we set roughly to discover what this announcement way and to choose whether to simply acknowledge or dismiss it, we'd be occupied with intuition which, for absence of a superior timeframe, we will call basic pondering. On the off chance that one wants to state that that is best a state of issue fixing in which the explanation is to choose whether or not or now not what's said is trustworthy, we won't thing. be that as it may, for our capacities we choose to call it vital pondering.

Adding a regulating issue to this idea, Ennis characterized urgent addressing as "the exact evaluating of proclamations" On the reason of this definition, he remarkable 12 "components" of critical pondering like sorts or components of explanations, which incorporate making a decision about whether a perception revelation is solid and getting a handle on the significance of a presentation. He alluded to that he did never again incorporate making a decision about worth articulations. straightforward over the 12 viewpoints, he exceptional three elements of basic addressing: legitimate (making a decision about connections among implications of expressions and proclamations), criterial (know-how of the criteria for passing judgment on explanations), and down to business (the impression of the foundation intention). For every perspective, Ennis depicted the appropriate measurements, including criteria. He proposed the subsequent amass as an establishment for creating specs for basic addressing checks and for thinks about on scholarly methodologies and levels.

In the Nineteen Seventies and Eighties there was an upsurge important to the improvement of pondering abilities. the yearly worldwide gathering on significant pondering and scholarly Reform has pulled in since its beginning in 1980 a huge number of instructors.

Introduction

Basic reasoning is independently directed, self-trained reasoning which endeavors to reason at the most significant level of value in an honest manner. Individuals who think basically reliably endeavor to live objectively, sensibly, empathically. They are distinctly mindful of the characteristically defective nature of human reasoning when left unchecked. They endeavor to reduce the intensity of their egocentric and sociocentric inclinations. They utilize the scholarly devices that basic reasoning offers – ideas and rules that empower them to break down, survey, and improve thinking. They work steadily to build up the scholarly temperance's of scholarly uprightness, scholarly modesty, scholarly consideration, scholarly sympathy, scholarly feeling of equity and trust in reason. They understand that regardless of how talented they are as scholars, they can generally improve their thinking capacities and they will on occasion fall prey to botches in thinking, human unreasonableness, preferences, predispositions, mutilations, uncritically acknowledged social standards and taboos, personal circumstance, and personal stake. They endeavor to improve the world in the manners they can and add to an increasingly reasonable, enlightened society. Simultaneously, they perceive the complexities frequently inborn in doing as such. They abstain from contemplating entangled issues and endeavor to fittingly think about the rights and needs of significant others. They perceive the complexities in creating as scholars, and invest in long lasting practice toward personal growth. They encapsulate the Socratic standard: The unexamined life does not merit living, in light of the fact that they understand that numerous unexamined lives respectively bring about an uncritical, low, risky world.

Essential thinking is that the examination of assurances to frame a judgment. The subject is exceptional, and some particular definitions exist, that for the chief half fuse the fair, far-fetched, unprejudiced assessment, or evaluation of right confirmation. Essential thinking is independently directed, self-prepared, self-watched, and self-healing thinking. It expect agree to intensive checks of enormity and cautious course of their usage. It includes ground-breaking correspondence and requesting thinking limits even as and assurance to beat local egotism and sociocentrism.

Hypothetical Domain

Hypothetical basic reasoning includes helping the understudy build up a thankfulness for logical clarifications of conduct. This implies learning the substance of brain science as well as how and why brain research is sorted out into ideas, standards, laws, and speculations. Creating hypothetical aptitudes starts in the early on course where the essential basic reasoning goal is understanding and applying ideas suitably. For instance, when you acquaint understudies with the standards of fortification, you can solicit them to discover models from the standards in the news or to make up stories that show the standards.

Mid-level courses in the major require more complexity, moving understudies past use of ideas and standards to learning and applying hypotheses. For example, you can give a rich contextual analysis in irregular brain research and solicit understudies to bode well from the case from alternate points of view, underlining hy pothetical adaptability or precise utilization of existing and acknowledged systems in brain science to clarify examples of conduct. In cutting edge courses we can reasonably request that understudies assess hypothesis, choosing the most valuable or dismissing the least supportive. For instance, understudies can differentiate various models to clarify illicit drug use in physiological brain science. By looking at the qualities and shortcomings of existing systems, they can choose which hypotheses serve best as they figure out how to legitimize their reactions dependent on proof and reason.

Capstone, praises, and graduate courses go past hypothesis assessment to urge understudies to make hypothesis. Understudies select an intricate inquiry concerning conduct (for instance, recognizing instruments that underlie chemical imbalance or language procurement) and build up their own hypothesis based clarifications for the conduct. This test expects them to orchestrate and coordinate existing hypothesis just as devise new bits of knowledge into the conduct.

Present brain research as an open-finished, developing endeavor. Understudies regularly imagine that their entrance into the control speaks to an end-point where everything great and genuine has just been found. That end supports lack of involvement instead of criticality. Point out that examination is brain science' s method for developing and creating. Each new disclosure in brain research speaks to a conceivably rich demonstration of basic reasoning. A ton of space for disclosure remains. New thoughts will be created and old originations disposed of.Require understudy execution that goes past remembrance. Gathering work, expositions, discusses, subjects, letters to well known therapists, diaries, recent development models these and more can be utilized as a methods for building up the higher abilities associated with basic speculation in brain science. Find broken reason impact ends in the sensationalist newspapers. Solicit understudies to recognize what sorts from proof would warrant faith in business claims. In spite of the fact that it is troublesome, even all around structured target test things can catch basic reasoning aptitudes with the goal that understudies are tested past insignificant reiteration and review.

Explain your assumptions regarding execution with express, open criteria. Formulating clear execution criteria for brain science activities will upgrade understudy achievement. Understudies frequently grumble that they don't comprehend "what you need" when you appoint work. Execution criteria determine the gauges that you will use to assess their work. For instance, perfonnance criteria for the perception practice depicted before might incorporate the accompanying: The understudy portrays conduct precisely; offers derivation that is sensible for the specific circumstance; and recognizes individual factors that may impact deduction. Perfonnance criteria encourage giving itemized criticism effectively and can likewise advance understudy self-evaluation.

Support a scrutinizing mentality. Understudies regularly accept that on the off chance that they have inquiries regarding their perusing, at that point they are some way or another being shameful, inconsiderate, or dumb. Having dialogs right off the bat in the course about the job of good inquiries in upgrading the nature of the subject and extending the sharpness of the brain may set a progressively basic stage on which understudies can play. Model basic speculation from certain bits of knowledge you have had about conduct or from some examination you have directed previously. Compliment understudies who offer genuine instances of the standards under investigation. Thank understudies who ask idea related inquiries and portray for what good reason you think their inquiries are great. Leave existence for additional. Your own energy about basic reasoning can be an extraordinary motivator for understudies to look for that fervor.

Basic Thinking in Everyday Life

Have you at any point been tuning in to one of your educator's exercises and felt that it had no significance to your own life? You're not the only one. Pretty much every understudy has felt a similar way. Without a doubt, you utilize basic speculation abilities in the homeroom to take care of word issues in math, compose papers in English, and make theories in science.

Be that as it may, by what method will you utilize basic speculation in regular day to day existence? To start with, remember that basic reasoning is essentially an "intentional manner of thinking."

Fundamentally, it implies that you are utilizing reason and rationale to reach a decision about an issue or choice you are going head to head with. What's more, clear, stable thinking is something that will help you consistently. To assist you with making the jump from study hall to genuine world, here are 3 solid instances of basic intuition in regular day to day existence.

Counterfeit News versus Genuine News

Pause for a minute to think about your media aptitudes. Do you think you have the stuff to sift through a genuine news source from a bit of cunning promoting? As indicated by an ongoing report from Stanford University, an astounding 82% of the teenagers overviewed couldn't recognize a promotion named "supported substance" and a real news story.

Some portion of the issue may return from schools cutting on formal guidance of basic reasoning aptitudes and a suspicion that the present "advanced local" youngsters can naturally differentiate without training or guidance. You are great at bunches of things. Be that as it may, you know, you've drilled those things you're great at. All in all, how might you work on telling actuality from fiction?

One way (outside of school) is to talk with your loved ones about media sources. Discover how they remain educated, and why they pick those outlets. Approach each other routine inquiries for assessing sources.

Do your Friends Know Everything?

It's enticing to accept that the world starts and finishes with your companions. Try not to misunderstand me. Companions are certainly significant. Be that as it may, it pays to mirror a little on how a gathering impacts our lives.

To rehearse basic deduction in regular day to day existence, investigate your gathering of companions. Are there things that are "prohibited" in your group of friends? It is safe to say that you are required to act a specific way, dress a specific way?

Think a specific way?

It's characteristic that when a gathering characterizes something as "cool", every one of the individuals in the gathering work to fit into that definition. Notwithstanding what they separately accept. The issue is that for all intents and purposes each circumstance can be characterized in numerous manners. What is "stupidity" to one individual can be "fine" to another. Build up your capacity to rethink the manner in which you see your general surroundings. All alone terms.

Discover when your companion bunch sees the negative in a circumstance. Is there a positive method to see it? Or if nothing else a way that causes it to appear not exactly so awful? You may not be prepared to make some noise with your autonomous view. What's more, that is alright. Simply work on deduction uniquely in contrast to the gathering to fortify your psyche.

Basic Thinking in the Driver's Seat

One of the center basic reasoning aptitudes you need each day is the capacity to look at the suggestions and results of a conviction or activity. In its most profound structure, this capacity can assist you with shaping your very own arrangement of convictions in everything from environmental change to religion. Be that as it may, this aptitude can likewise spare your life (and your vehicle protection rate) in the driver's seat.

Envision you are cruising down the interstate when your telephone cautions you to an approaching instant message. The capacity to look at your latent capacity activities and their going with outcomes will assist you with settling on the best decision for how to deal with the circumstance.

Do you take a gander at the content and hazard getting into a mishap? Do you pause and hazard not reacting to a pressing issue? Or on the other hand do you destroy over to take a gander at the content and hazard being late for your arrangement? A similar expertise can be applied when you are searching for a spot to stop, when to pull onto a bustling road, or whether to run the yellow light. Even better, the more rehearsed you are at taking a gander at the ramifications of your driving propensities, the quicker you can settle on split second choices in the driver's seat.

Why crucial Thinking in lifestyle Matters

Actually everyone will profit by basic reasoning in lightweight of the very fact that the necessity for its close US. In a philosophical paper, Peter Facione puts forth a solid defense that basic reasoning aptitudes are needed by everyone, altogether social orders United Nations agency esteem well-being, equity, and an oversized cluster of alternative positive qualities:

"Considered as a sort of perceptive judgment or intelligent basic leadership, undeniably basic reasoning is ineluctable. There's not very an amount or a spot wherever it'd not seem to be of potential value. For no matter length of your time that people have functions at the highest of the priority list and need to pass judgment on the foremost skilled methodology to realize them, to that degree as people surprise what's valid and what is not, what to just accept and what to dismiss, solid basic reasoning are going to be basic." Along these lines, as such, as long as you keep inquisitive, deliberate, and goal-oriented, in spite of what your inclinations, you are going to need basic intuition to really possess your life.

Why essential Thinking Matters in Your Business

It is the desire for specialists to chase when occupations they're vivacious in regards to. Though finding indescribable paradise and importance from one's work is useful for benefit, it's basic to ensure extraordinary sentiments and main impetuses don't cloud fundamental instinct inside the working environment. Experts should use essential hypothesis by and large segments of working surroundings exercises to deal with a vital good ways from extortionate mistakes. From enlistment to displaying and arrangements, each definitive division needs to underline practicing fundamental hypothesis in work surroundings choices.

Jen Lawrence, co-maker of have collaboration the Fox: A Business Fable in regards to Thinking Critically and Motivating Your Team, portrays fundamental hypothesis as "the capacity to require care of issues feasibly by intentionally gathering data in regards to a trouble, fabricating more musings together with Associate in Nursing combination of purposes of read, surveying the information using clarification, and ensuring everybody identified with arranged."

This is a stunning definition for a perplexing arrangement. In spite of the undeniable reality that it will appear as simple as wandering back and using a standard hypothesis strategy as basic reacting naturally to conflicts or issues, this can be harder than one would conceivably anticipate. Fundamental thinking abilities will and should be instructed inside the work environment so they become normal. Essential thinking is significant in light-weight of the established truth that it ensures you have the best reaction to a trouble, with most outrageous buy in from all social occasions encased – an outcome which can in the end save your business time, cash and stress. Here's the style by that to handle, grasp and realize fundamental instinct in your working environment.

Showing basic deduction in the work environment

David Welton, overseeing accomplice at Grove Critical Thinking, says basic reasoning is "an open to instruction expertise." He takes note of that basic reasoning is regularly miscategorized as a delicate ability, however delicate aptitudes are not assertive. On the off chance that businesses and workers the same don't think basic reasoning is assertive, it is simple for it to be left by the wayside.

Both Lawrence and Welton suggest investigating basic reasoning trainings and strategies to improve your work environment's general basic reasoning capability. Those in official and administrative positions can start with an evaluation of which regions of the work environment appear to be generally ailing in basic reasoning.

In the event that mix-ups are reliably being made, it is useful to initially investigate whether the issue is an absence of basic reasoning, not an intrinsic issue with a representative or gathering of workers. At that point, you can examine what trainings, mentors or educational plans may accommodate your association best begin rehearsing straightforward hypothesis as a predilection with littler issues as fashions, and in a while stir your manner up to larger troubles," Lawrence aforementioned. Basic reasoning is tied in with tackling issues through discerning procedures and proof based information. Like the logical technique, basic reasoning contains a ton of steps, as Lawrence noted in her definition, yet these means will spare a great deal of time over the long haul if missteps can be forestalled.

Moving toward issues with a free, intelligent manner of thinking is one sort of basic reasoning. Basic reasoning structures contentions from proof, while naming issues and suspicions that can hinder assessing an issue for what it is. It's tied in with taking

care of issues in a procedure focused way that benefits from information and target proof – and in the business world, these abilities set aside time and cash start to finish. Not exclusively will it spare your business expensive assets, yet basic reasoning will likewise improve other working environment abilities, for example, correspondence, imagination, logical competency, enthusiastic knowledge and general critical thinking.

Setting aside time and cash with basic reasoning

A 24-hour sequence of media reports and flood of unchecked certainties over -burdens our minds all through the working environment. Lawrence said this adds to a hysterical working environment rhythm that fortifies hurried reasoning and business choices. This is when expensive mix-ups and bumbles are made.

Welton included that basic reasoning makes people better scholars, yet better communicators. Within the occasion that you simply will think all of the additional signally and higher fluent your positions, you'll be able to all the extra likely connect with talks and construct a notably additional vital dedication in your pastime." It may appear to be nonsensical to connect expository levelheadedness with passionate, significant commitment, yet when you can feel certain and careful in your basic leadership process, the final product will feel additionally satisfying and yield enthusiastic insight.

Much the same as basic reasoning procedures themselves, instructing and executing basic reasoning preparing and philosophy requires some investment and tolerance. Lawrence underlined that basic reasoning abilities are best procured in a period of quiet. It may feel earnest to search out basic speculation during an emergency, yet it is a hard aptitude to learn in a frenzy. Basic reasoning preparing is best done preemptively – that way, when an emergency hits, representatives will be readied and basic reasoning will work out easily.

From an official or administrative point of view, giving workers additional time on ventures or tackling issues may feel like a stressor if there are cutoff times or weights from higher up. Yet, in the event that you need those working for you to take part in basic reasoning procedures, it's basic to give them an opportunity to do as such. Once more, a portion of the pressure can be maintained a strategic distance from if basic reasoning is instructed preemptively, not if all else fails. Giving workers this additional time will really spare the organization time and cash over the long haul.

Distinguishing effective basic reasoning

Showing representatives basic deduction in the working environment enables them to utilize the expertise as an emergency occurs, not sometime later. Lawrence gave a model including eateries and waitstaff: If a client has an awful involvement with an eatery, a server utilizing basic reasoning aptitudes will be bound to make sense of an answer for spare the association, for example, offering a free canapé or rebate. "This could spare the nicely-deserved client qualitative analysis you spent a unbelievable deal of showcasing greenbacks to form."

This idea is appropriate crosswise over numerous business and hierarchical structures. While the café model passes on basic reasoning abilities, you ought to likewise know about the indications of an absence of those aptitudes. Organizations that change system quickly, moving starting with one thing then onto the next, are likely not participating in basic reasoning, said Lawrence. This is additionally the situation in organizations that appear to experience smart thoughts however experience issues executing them.

Likewise with numerous issues in business, what's going on at the top is a decent signifier of how present basic believing is in the remainder of the association. On the off chance that an organization has a shrewd pioneer with good thoughts yet no procedures being pursued, there will be no upfront investment, and the organization will endure. This is the reason basic reasoning abilities regularly go with positive relational abilities.

"Basic reasoning wouldn't while not a doubt assist you with landing at the high-quality answer, but at an answer a motivating several humans grasp," aforementioned Lawrence.Displaying basic intuition at the top will enable the ability to stream down to the remainder of the association, regardless of what kind or size of organization you have. At the point when missteps are kept away from and business is consistent at all levels, not exactly at the official level that implies basic reasoning is effectively executed in an association. Between trainings, time and persistence, basic reasoning can turn into a natural aptitude for representatives at all degrees of experience and position. The cash, time and strife you will spare over the long haul is certainly justified regardless of the additional time and persistence of actualizing basic intuition in your working environment.

The Skills we'd like for vital Thinking

The abilities that we'd like thus on have the choice to suppose basically square measure shifted and incorporate perception, investigation, elucidation, reflection, assessment, derivation, clarification, vital thinking, and basic leadership.

Explicitly we must always have the choice to:

Consider an issue or issue in an exceedingly target and basic manner.

- Recognize the varied contentions there square measure in association to a selected issue.

- Assess a degree of read to choose however solid or substantial it's.

- Perceive any shortcomings or negative focuses that there square measure within the proof or competition.

- Notice what suggestions there could also be behind Associate in Nursing announcement or competition.

- Give organized thinking and backing to a competition that we tend to want to create.

The important Thinking method

You got to understand that none people assume primarily perpetually. Some of the time we expect in much any manner nonetheless basically, as an example once our poise is influenced by outrage, pain or elation or once we area unit feeling out and out 'ridiculous disapproved'. Then again, as luck would have it, since our basic reasoning capability fluctuates as per our gift mentality, additional usually than not we will understand a way to improve our basic intuition capability by buildup sure commonplace exercises and applying them to all or any problems that gift themselves. When you comprehend the hypothesis of basic reasoning, up your basic reasoning aptitudes takes purpose and follow.

What are you progressing to Achieve?

One of the foremost vital components of basic basic cognitive process is to {settle onto decide on} what you're expecting to accomplish and later on settle on a selection addicted to a scope of conceivable outcomes.

When you have explained that specialize in yourself you must utilize it because the starting stage in each single future circumstance requiring thought and, perhaps, additional basic leadership. Wherever needed, build your coworkers, family or folks around you conscious of your goal to hunt once this objective. You must then teach yourself to stay heading in the right direction till dynamical conditions mean you wish to come back to the start of the fundamental leadership method.

In any case, there are things that hinder basic leadership. we have a tendency to as a full convey with North American nation a scope of various preferences, learnt practices and individual inclinations created for the length of our lives; they're the signs of being human. A big commitment to guaranteeing we predict primarily is to grasp concerning these individual attributes, inclinations and predispositions and provide leniency for them whereas brooding about conceivable resultant stages, notwithstanding whether or not they are at the pre-activity thought organize or as an element of a rethink caused by surprising or unexpected obstructions to proceed with progress.

The additional clearly we all know concerning ourselves, our qualities and shortcomings, the virtually sure our basic reasoning are going to be paid.

The Benefit of Foresight

Maybe the most significant component of reasoning basically is prescience. Practically all choices we make and actualize don't demonstrate sad on the off chance that we discover motivations to relinquish them. Notwithstanding, our basic leadership will be limitlessly better and bound to prompt achievement if, when we arrive at a speculative resolution, we stop and think about the effect on the individuals and exercises around us.

The components requiring thought are commonly various and shifted. As a rule, thought of one component from an alternate point of view will uncover potential perils in seeking after our choice.

For example, moving a business action to another area may improve potential yield extensively yet it might likewise prompt the loss of gifted laborers if the separation moved is excessively incredible. Which of these is the more significant thought? Is there some method for diminishing the contention? These are the kind of issues that may emerge from deficient basic reasoning, a showing maybe of the basic significance of good basic reasoning.

For what reason Do Employers worth vital Thinking Skills?

Bosses would like work up-and-comers United Nations agency will assess a circumstance utilizing legitimate plan and supply the simplest arrangement. Basic reasoning capacities area unit among the foremost searched for once talents in just about each business and dealing setting. You'll be able to show basic deduction by utilizing connected catchphrases in your resume and introductory letter, and through your meeting.

Instances of vital Thinking

The conditions that request basic intuition disagree from business to business. A couple of models include:

- A sorting nurture dissects the present cases and chooses the request by that the patients need to be forbidden.

- A fixer assesses the materials that might best suit a particular activity.

- An attorney audits proof and devises a procedure to win a case or to settle on whether or not to in camera address any remaining problems.

- A chief examines shopper criticism structures and uses this knowledge to create up a shopper care tutorial meeting for representatives.

Advance Your Skills in Your Job Search

On the off likelihood that essential thinking might be a key articulation inside the movement postings you're applying for, guarantee to underscore your fundamental instinct abilities at some phase in your quest for work.

Add Keywords to Your Resume

You can use fundamental thinking catchphrases (descriptive, basic reasoning, inventiveness, and afterward forward.) in your resume. While depiction your work history, consolidate any of the aptitudes recorded underneath that precisely delineate you. You'll have the option to in like manner remember them for your resume summation, on the off likelihood that you basically have one.

For example, your framework may analyze, "Publicizing go with 5 years of inclusion with adventure the board. Capable in directing cautious applied math mensuration and challenger assessment to gauge feature examples and customer needs, and to make right verifying ways."

Notice Skills in Your message

Recollect these essential theory aptitudes for you're early on letter. Inside the body of your letter, notice a bunch of those aptitudes, and gives express examples of times after you have demonstrated those abilities at work. Consider times after you required to analyze or evaluate materials to require care of a trouble.

Show the querier Your Skills

You can utilize these power words in an exceedingly meeting. Mention after you were looked with a selected issue or challenge at work and clarify however you applied basic speculation to know it.

A few questioners can offer you a speculative state of affairs or issue, and request that you simply utilize basic intuition skills to know it. For this case, clarify your perspective altogether to the verbalizer. The person is generally more and more targeted around however you land at your answer as hostile the arrangement itself. The verbalizer must see you utilize investigation and assessment (key items of basic intuition) thanks to take care of the given state of affairs or issue.

Obviously, every activity would require varied aptitudes and encounters, therefore make sure you scan the set of operating responsibilities cautiously and focus on the talents recorded by the business.

Top Critical Thinking Skills

Examination

Some portion of basic reasoning is the capacity to deliberately look at something, regardless of whether it is an issue, a lot of information, or a book. Individuals with

scientific aptitudes can analyze data, comprehend what it implies, and appropriately disclose to others the ramifications of that data.

- Posing Thoughtful Inquiries.

- Information Analysis.

- Research.

- Elucidation.

- Judgment.

- Addressing Evidence.

- Perceiving Patterns.

- Distrust.

Correspondence

Regularly, you should impart your decisions to your bosses or with a gathering of associates. You should have the option to speak with others to share your thoughts viably. You may likewise need to draw in basic deduction in a gathering. For this situation, you should work with others and impart viably to make sense of answers for complex issues.

- Undivided attention.

- Appraisal.

- Coordinated effort.

- Clarification.

- Relational.

- Introduction.

- Cooperation.

- Verbal Communication.

- Composed Communication

Inventiveness

Basic reasoning frequently includes imagination and development. You may need to spot designs in the data you are taking a gander at or concoct an answer that nobody else has thought of previously. The entirety of this includes an inventive eye that can adopt an alternate strategy from every different methodologies.

- Adaptability.

- Conceptualization.

- Interest.

- Creative mind.

- Drawing Connections.

- Inducing.

- Foreseeing.

- Incorporating.

- Vision.

Liberality

To think fundamentally, you should have the option to set aside any suppositions or decisions and only dissect the data you get. You should be objective, assessing thoughts without predisposition.

- Assorted variety.

- Reasonableness.

- Lowliness.

- Comprehensive.

- Objectivity.

- Perception.

- Reflection

Ways to Think More Critically

Presently we go to the part that I'm certain you've all been hanging tight for: how the hell improve at basic reasoning? Underneath, you'll discover seven different ways to begin.

1. Pose Basic Inquiries

Once in a while a clarification turns out to be unpredictable to the point that the first question get lost. To keep away from this, ceaselessly return to the essential inquiries you posed to when you set out to take care of the issue. Here are a couple of key essential inquiry you can pose to when moving toward any issue:

- What do you definitely know?

- How would you realize that?

- What are you attempting to demonstrate, negate, illustrated, study, and so on.

- What are you disregarding?

Probably the most amazing answers for issues are bewildering not due to their unpredictability, but since of their exquisite straightforwardness. Look for the straightforward arrangement first.

2. Question Basic Assumptions

The higher than discourse correspondence stays consistent once you're completely pondering a difficulty. It's completely straightforward to form Associate in nursing ass of yourself primarily by fail to research your essential assumptions. Likely the most effective pioneers in humanity's history were the people UN agency simply researched for a second and considered whether or not one amongst everyone's general doubts wasn't right., tending to doubts is that the spot progression happens.

You ought not to be unnatural to be a cheerful Einstein to learn by work your assumptions. That outing you have got needed to take? That recreation action you have got needed to endeavor? That section level position you have got needed to get? That attractive individual in your World Civilizations classification you have got needed to speak with?

All of these things are a reality within the occasion merely that you just} primarily question your assumptions and primarily measure your feelings with reference to what's affordable, fitting, or attainable. On the off chance that you just are looking for some help with this strategy, around then confirm the standing of Oblique methods. It's Associate in nursing instrument that performing artist Brian Enno and trained worker Peter national pioneer created to assist originative imperative reasoning. a small indefinite quantity little bit of the "cards" zone unit specific to music, all things thought-about most work for at no matter purpose you're stuck on a difficulty.

3. Understand Your Mental Processes

Human plan is astounding, nonetheless the speed and mechanization with that it happens will be a damage once we're making an attempt to suppose essentially. Our minds ordinarily North American nation heuristics (mental straightforward routes) to clarify what is going on on around us. This was valuable to folks once we were chasing monumental game and heading off wild creatures, but it o.k. could also be heartrending once we're making an attempt to decide on UN agency to choose in favor of.

A basic scholar is aware of concerning their psychological inclinations and individual partialities and the way they impact apparently "objective" selections and arrangements. We all have predispositions in our reasoning. Obtaining aware of them is that the factor that produces basic reasoning conceivable.

4. Have a go at Reversing Things

An extraordinary method to get "unstuck" on a difficult issue is to have a go at turning around things. It might appear glaringly evident that X causes Y, however imagine a scenario in which Y caused X.

The "chicken and egg issue" an exemplary case of this. From the start, it appears glaringly evident that the chicken needed to start things out. The chicken lays the egg, all things considered. Yet, at that point you rapidly understand that the chicken needed to originate from some place, and since chickens originate from eggs, the egg more likely than not start things out. Or on the other hand did it.Regardless of whether things being what they are, the turnaround isn't valid, thinking of it as can show you the way to finding an answer.

5. Assess the Existing Evidence

At the point when you're attempting to take care of an issue, it's constantly useful to take a gander at other work that has been done in a similar region. There's no motivation to
begin tackling an issue without any preparation when somebody has laid the foundation.

It's significant, be that as it may, to assess this data basically, or else you can without much of a stretch arrive at an inappropriate resolution. Pose the accompanying inquiries of any proof you experience:

- Who assembled this proof?

- How could they assemble it?

- Why?

Take, for instance, an examination demonstrating the medical advantages of a sugary grain. On paper, the investigation sounds truly persuading. That is, until you discover that a sugary oat organization financed it.You can't consequently accept this negates the examination's outcomes, however you ought to surely address them when an irreconcilable circumstance is so evident.

6. Make sure to think for yourself

Try not to get so impeded in research and perusing that you neglect to think for yourself–now and again this can be your most amazing asset. Expounding on Einstein's paper "On the Electrodynamics of Moving Bodies" (the paper that contained the celebrated condition E=mc2), C.P. Under the hundred "Maybein Einstein" range Goth Safgord was the Wolf under the standard of earnest money, freelance, his not -so-Movement in his Check-out. To an amazingly colossal degree, that is actually what he had done.

Try not to be arrogant, yet perceive that deduction for yourself is fundamental to responding to extreme inquiries. I see this as evident when composing papers it's so natural to lose all sense of direction in others' work that I neglect to have my own considerations. Try not to commit this error.

Critical Thinking

CHAPTER 2

Improve Your Problem Solving

What are crucial thinking talents and for what reason are they important

Critical thinking is AN all-inclusive activity ability that applies to any position and every trade. Whereas everyone is entrusted with some kind of crucial thinking in their operating atmosphere, not all representatives are nice at it.

Understanding the essential components engaged with crucial thinking can assist you with rising this vary of talents and exhibit your ability to businesses. Solid issue solvers are a big growth to any cluster.

The four phases of crucial thinking

You can utilize a good vary of how to touch upon crucial thinking, nonetheless you may commonly go through four clear stages in spite of what course you're taking. Seeing every progression of the procedure can assist you with sharpening your concern aptitudes to all or any them a lot of possible serve you on your journey toward a shrewd, useful arrangement.

Characterize the difficulty: establish the issue that you are managing. Watch the difficulty territory close to structure a natty gritty image of what is up. Examine representative conduct, operating atmosphere ways, and dealing methodology. Maintain your stress on the difficulty currently, and fight the temptation to characterize the difficulty as way as a solution. As an example, "We have to be compelled to improve getting ready methods" addresses the arrangement quite the difficulty. "Deals documentation is conflicting" higher characterizes the difficulty.

Conceptualize options: this can be one among the foremost important phases of crucial thinking. It needs a cautious parity of originality and legit reasoning. Scrutinize all potential alternative choices. Break down the money, time, staff, and assets basic for every approach even as the arrival that you simply will anticipate from completely different techniques.

Pick the most effective procedure: sturdy basic leadership is prime at this stage. When cautiously considering the whole thing of your alternatives, you must opt for the most effective procedure for your concern and keep on with your call. Employees World Health Organization falter or battle to specialize in a solitary arrangement do not create nice issue solvers since they stall out at this basic purpose all the whereas.

Execute your answer: Implementation is that the basic pinnacle of the crucial thinking method. This can be the place you draw up AN activity arrange, share it with the correct school, and end your picked methodology.

Fundamental aptitudes for fruitful essential thinking

Critical thinking could seem to be clear from the offset, nonetheless there are varied representatives WHO bumble quite a minimum of one in ev ery of the essential advances, neglecting to effectively resolve operating setting problems. Effective essential thinking needs many important aptitudes that may assist you with continued profitably from identifying proof to usage.

In the starting times of essential thinking, you have got to own solid data-based talents. As opposition tolerating problems at face esteem, you have got to indicate sidelong reasoning and logical capacities. These can assist you fittingly valuate what is happening and pinpoint the middle reason for the difficulty.

As you investigate potential answers for the difficulty, you must exhibit constancy. Finding the proper thanks to touch upon the difficulty will not return effectively. Inventive reasoning can work well for you. Representatives WHO understand a way to use their inventive reasoning offices can exceed expectations within the second and third phases of essential thinking, as they are able to concoct approaches that others have unnoticed.

Actualizing your answer needs its own vary of talents. This usually needs a cautious parity of cooperation and initiative. You'll need to exhibit skillfulness to face up to ineluctable pushback from associates WHO oppose modification. Each correspondence and exchange are important currently. once you've got actualized your answer, you'll need to use basic reasoning and scrupulousness as you survey the outcomes and alter your technique varied to confirm the difficulty is effectively settled.

Sharpening crucial thinking talents

Critical thinking talents square measure vital in every trade. There isn't any business that's safe to the customary assault of problems. Business directors and workplace administrators could notice that regarding every a part of their day schedule bases on some style of crucial thinking. At the purpose once you are in AN administration position, one amongst the foremost vital belongings you do is actually handle the everyday problems that emerge for your representatives.

Improving your crucial thinking talents can offer you A clear edge each in AN administration work and in several things within your organization. You'll be able to sharpen your crucial thinking aptitudes by:

Working on conceptualizing exercises, for instance, mind mapping.

- Moving toward standard problems with AN "imagine a state of affairs in which" angle, systematically testing new approaches.

- Keeping an inspiration diary wherever you write down the whole lot of your thoughts, no matter however out-of-the-container.

- Working through principle riddles and games like Sudoku. Following trade productions covering the foremost recent programming and procedures for basic problems.

Exhibiting essential thinking on your resume

Bosses rummage around for new contracts World Health Organization have shown essential thinking aptitudes. It's too little to only state "critical thinking abilities" on your resume. You have got to represent exactly what varieties of issue aptitudes at that you exceed expectations and show express instances of however you've got used these talents in past positions.

At the purpose once you are exhibiting your essential thinking talents on a resume, you have to be compelled to compactly observe of however you recognized the problem, engineered up a solution, and existent this system.

A few instances of solid essential thinking explanations include:

- Decreased security infringement thirty % by introducing deliberately place railings on the generation floor.

- Expanded client loyalty appraisals twenty % by growing new contents to handle traditional inquiries.

- Cut delivery prices by ten % quarterly with changed programming arrangements.

Clarify that you simply saw a problem pertinent to your specialty, found an inventive technique to fathom it, and accomplished quantitative outcomes together with your picked methodology. Showing essential thinking is important despite what position you are applying for. In shopper help, you issue comprehend anytime you manage a hard shopper. As a comptroller, you are essential thinking approaches to cut back expenses and raise financial gain. Written agreement employees illuminate problems that emerge once a customer's solicitations seem to be impossible for the given development house. You are typically essential thinking. Guarantee potential businesses will see that you are nice at it.

Critical thinking aptitudes square measure as differed because the problems they are applied to. withal, all the most effective issue solvers use an identical essential thanks to handle distinctive and taking care of problems, fusing the aptitudes documented here to use victories. Make sure you track your essential thinking victories, live the results, and incorporate these on your resume therefore accomplishment supervisors can expertise no problem distinctive you as a solid issue convergent thinker.

Building essential Thinking Skills to unravel issues at Work

Pursue this six-advance dialog procedure to cultivate basic intuition in your cluster.

Basic reasoning may be a crucial delicate ability for associate association's prosperity. Have a go at following this six-advance essential thinking method along with your cluster to fabricate and utilize this ability. One of the most difficulties that organizations face within the returning decade is that the utilization of basic deduction talents within the work surroundings. The capability to utilize information from an additional in depth associated more and more color-blind purpose of read offers your representatives an approach to decide on progressively educated selections and what is more observe a so much reaching perspective on any circumstance. The U.S. Branch of Labor has as currently recognized basic speculation as a crude material for a few crucial work surroundings aptitudes, together with essential thinking and basic leadership.

Organizations have perceived the necessity for incorporating this delicate ability into the operating surroundings to assist fabricate the action of their associations. As indicated by associate current Wall Street Journal article, associate examination by so.com found that notices for basic speculation in work postings have increased since 2009. This audit is upheld by the yank Management Association essential Skills Survey that found that over seventy plc. of taking associate interest directors distinguished basic speculation as an important part of representative advancement.

Basic reasoning assists individuals with taking a goose at circumstances from numerous sides, and later on envision some distinct approaches to react. This open procedure of reasoning presents thoughts and arrangements that stretch the open doors for progress. One in all the elemental reasons organizations do not hold onto basic intuition as a basic piece of their association is that they believe they're merely overly occupied. The stress on everyday tasks and profit development takes want over actualizing this delicate experience. In any case, organizations that build up this ability will see associate growth in cooperation and gain, and a decrease in strife. These end of the day advantages exceed the time place resources into cultivating the ability. You'll consolidate exercises into the workday that coordinate basic intuition while not utilizing outside getting ready programs.

Here may be an essential thinking method for cluster collection that grows the use of basic intuition for your representatives.

Name the circumstance.

At the point when you name the circumstance, you present a solitary talk point that everybody in the dialog can distinguish. This announcement can be composed on a whiteboard as a visual brief with the goal that everybody in the group maintains the emphasis on the point, diverting the dialog to the point of convergence when the subject movements. Basic reasoning includes keeping a receptive outlook about circumstances. You assist members with recalling the objective of the gathering by naming the circumstance.

Rundown every single imaginable arrangement.

Conceptualizing happens during this piece of the procedure. There is nothing outside the domain of conceivable outcomes now in the dialog. At the point when you open the discussion to boundless alternatives, you extend thinking past one individual. The capacity to extend your reasoning offers the discussion numerous potential arrangements that you might not have considered without the outflow of considerations and feelings. Ensure that every potential arrangement talked about during this time remain focused for the circumstance that has been named in stage one. Basic reasoning incorporates the capacity to keep a receptive outlook to different contemplations and perspectives without forgetting about the ultimate objective. You extend the dialog to see new choices and furthermore keep focused by recognizing different chances.

Restricted your answers for three choices.

Everybody in the group needs to concur with at any rate one of the three alternatives. People who can discover a tradeoff and make arrangements from numerous points of view are better ready to unite a group. Print every arrangement at the highest point of a whiteboard and compose beneath everyone a rundown of its favorable circumstances and impediments utilizing a discerning contention. Basic reasoning aptitudes offer the capacity to take a gander at circumstances objectively without decisions of good and terrible or off-base and right. You help keep a sound dialog set up when you carry agreement to a couple of deliberately picked arrangements.

Pick one selection from the 3 choices.

Settle on a final call that provides the foremost obvious chance with regards to progress concerning keen about captivated with obsessed with passionate about addicted to addicted to obsessed on smitten by} the even handed dialog about the circumstance.

Survey this call in affiliation to however well it takes care of the allotted issue. Basic reasoning skills assist individuals with utilizing an increasingly organized approach to succeed in resolutions. This diminishes the chance of selecting selections enthusiastic about mistaken deductions rising from perfervid ends.

Set up an instructions to complete the picked game plan.

Your picked plan must be constrained to have courses of occasions and a summarizing that recognizes that individuals territory unit answerable for what segments of the last game plan. Fundamental thinking aptitudes fuse the capacity to work in the picked course of action. You increase delicate I give it a second thought and energy from the individuals in capital punishment the game plan after they region unit a significant bit of the methodology.

Complete the arrangement.

A few workers discover this piece of the procedure the most troublesome. Think about the occasions an extraordinary arrangement struggled on the grounds that there was no development. Ensure every individual from the group has a section to play in the process that underlines their specialized topics and intrigue. Complete standard audits of individuals and courses of events for venture the board. Basic reasoning includes the capacity to see the estimation of the general arrangement. Now simultaneously, people ought to have the option to see the estimation of the arrangement and have purchase in since they were a piece of the procedure.

This critical thinking process makes a domain where basic reasoning turns into a working piece of finding an answer. For people who battle with this strategy, you might need to think about some preparation in basic reasoning. Generally, however, this procedure advances basic intuition in your representatives. You can likewise incorporate this movement for making arrangements and making a crucial. The worth added to your association incorporates improved commitment, understanding and efficiency from your group.

For what reason are basic reasoning and critical thinking basic in the present instruction

Basic reasoning methods having the option to exhibit proof for our thoughts, breaking down the manner in which we consider rather essentially learning realities while never addressing them. With regards to some school subjects, numerous individuals are persuaded that basic reasoning isn't fundamental, as the understudies ought to just depend on what they are told. There are numerous reasons, however, why accepting that critical thinking and basic reasoning are valuable in each school field.

1 – Students are being set up for employments that don't exist yet

The working environment is evolving quickly, and school needs to adjust to it. This implies tolerating we don't have the foggiest idea how the occupations of things to come will resemble. Basic reasoning and critical thinking are viewed as key aptitudes for this questionable future, particularly thinking about how remote work appears to turn out to be increasingly better known as the years pass by. Later on, laborers will be likely chosen dependent on their capacity to be autonomous from smaller scale overseeing and ready to work with less supervision and even away from the workplace.

2 -Basic reasoning improves understudies' adaptability and learning aptitudes

The present understudies are likely not to work utilizing similar apparatuses they are utilizing to think about. We don't have a clue how innovation will change when they will graduate, and learning basic reasoning will set them up to learn and adjust quicker and stay up with the latest with important changes in their fields of study, whatever they might be.

3 – Critical reasoning is the embodiment of majority rule government

Landon E. Beyer aforementioned "to live effectively in a very vote based mostly system, people should have the choice to suppose primarily therefore on choose trustworthy selections concerning near to home and municipal problems. In the event that understudies figure out how to think fundamentally, at that point they can utilize great deduction as the guide by which they live their lives."

4 – Critical reasoning makes Education not so much inactive but rather more intuitive Showing understudies how to move toward fundamentally any subject makes it progressively applicable for them. Now and again, particularly in youthful understudies, horrible showing can be clarified with a sentiment of separation from the subject and its significance in their lives. Making them feel as they are dynamic members could help taking care of this issue.

5 – Critical reasoning assists understudies with bettering express their thoughts Basic reasoning aptitudes are not restricted to a subject, and they can be applied to anything, from governmental issues to material science. The capacity of reasoning consistently and efficiently has an immense effect on how we get thoughts, however on how we express them. Regardless of whether we decide to be a history teacher or a researcher, having the option to clarify what we need and what are objectives in the best manner is a priceless aptitude, in the work environment just as throughout everyday life.

6 – Critical reasoning and critical thinking help making the cutting edge increasingly versatile to changes

The watchword to depict our future is "unsure", and our capacity to adjust will be now and again the main expertise we can utilize. Keeping a receptive outlook, having the option to self-immediate, self-control and self-screen, Legislative issues influences our lives regardless of how engaged with it we are, and basic reasoning will enable understudies to guarantee their choices depend on actualities and rationale.

10 ways that to enhance Your Problem -Solving Skills Critical thinking

While it's going to seem like some folks are merely brought into the planet with additional grounded essential thinking aptitudes, there are systems that anybody will use to enhance them.

Truth is trespasser than fiction, it's conceivable to basically improve your capacities here and therefore the better part is, the overwhelming majority of those exercises are to boot actually fun!

What are the various styles of Problem-Solving Skills

Before we tend to get to the fun exercises, we must always refine our comprehension of essential thinking talents that are any ways that assist you reliably:

- Comprehend the explanations for problems.

- Defeat fugitive emergencies.

- Make procedures to require care of long-term problems.

- Transform problems into opportunities.

You'll have the choice to require care of problems in your job higher as you develop in your industry-explicit info. Be that because it might, there are likewise some of general essential thinking aptitudes we tend to as an entire need:

- Characterizing the Problem: Deeply understanding a difficulty through analysis, prompting higher arrangements. Analysis will incorporate meeting, understanding books and messages, work cash connected info, ransacking through your association's computer network, and searching for your discoveries.

- Conceptualizing: making a bunch of recent arrangements speedily. In bunch conceptualizes, alter everyone to state thoughts. Welcome all information, and evade analysis. At that time, arranged arrangements into bunches around regular subjects.

- Dissecting: victimization trained manners of thinking to assess each conceivable arrangement. Aside from posting their expenses and benefits, you will apply deductive thinking, game hypothesis, and therefore the standards of principle (counting paradoxes) to them.

- Overseeing Risk: Anticipating and making an attempt to remain far away from the drawbacks of key arrangements. Your cluster will list potential dangers, rate however probably every is, foresee a date by that every may either occur or nevermore be a difficulty, and devise approaches to minimize those dangers.

- Choosing: The capability to decide on a solution and push ahead with it. Once an appropriate live of your time, Associate in Nursing investigation of potential arrangements, and criticism from colleagues, Associate in Nursing appointed decider should choose and actualize a solution.

- Overseeing Emotions: Applying spirited insight therefore on improve your and your colleagues' capability to assume plainly. This expects you to understand feelings in yourself furthermore as people, administer sentiments, and channel feelings into useful work.

Methodologies for Problem Solving

Basic reasoning is the procedure of objectively investigating and endeavoring to take care of an issue precisely and productively without depending on suppositions or estimates. For understudies, basic reasoning is a significant piece of the examination and learning forms. Business pioneers depend on basic speculation to assist them with tackling everyday issues, alongside major authoritative issues, at insignificant expense and as fast as could be expected under the circumstances.

Survey and Restate the Problem

One of the focal techniques to basic reasoning and critical thinking is creating as complete an understanding as conceivable of the issue. This implies repeating the issue in various manners to find out about its measurements, related issues, and where to search for data about the issue and potential arrangements. Evaluating an issue utilizing basic reasoning may uncover that it is anything but an issue by any means, or that it's difficult to unravel given current conditions, which enables a business head to concentrate on lessening its destructive impacts as opposed to scanning for a total arrangement.

Empower Creativity

While basic deduction centers around certainties and proof to take care of issues, this doesn't imply that it bars innovative idea and creative mind. Rather, basic deduction depends on issue solvers to think about various arrangements of potential arrangements before settling on choices and following up on them. An innovative critical thinking system may require working together with others to get new info or hear thoughts that you wouldn't consider alone. It might likewise expect you to be persistent while your thoughts create and develop.

Question Assumptions

Addressing suspicions is a significant system to utilize at each progression of the basic reasoning procedure. Because arrangements were compelling in the past doesn't mean they'll be among the most ideal arrangements now. Utilize your very own exploration as opposed to depending on data from questionable sources. Utilize numerous information focuses or contextual analyses to check the exactness and culmination of the data you gather. Regardless of whether scrutinizing a supposition doesn't make you dismiss it, it might in any case carry you more like a total comprehension of the best arrangements by enabling you to look at the issue from another perspective.

Development

The basic reasoning procedure shouldn't end once you select an answer for your concern and actualize it. Rather, exhaustive critical thinking stretches out the basic deduction procedure to incorporate a key follow-up that enables you to assess the result. You can contrast this with your anticipated outcomes of actualizing your answer, utilizing the data to recognize shortcomings in your basic reasoning procedure or quest for shockingly better arrangements.

8 interesting activities to supercharge your problem-fixing competencies

Use those ten creative tips to enhance hassle-solving abilities, expand extra strategic approaches of thinking, and teach your brain to do extra.

1. Dance your heart Out

Did you already know that dancing has an advantageous impact on neural processing, probable growing new neural pathways to go round dopamine-depleted blockages within the mind.

This means that in case you engage in ballet or every other shape of based dance, doing so may facilitate convergent thinking. In other phrases, it could assist you find an unmarried, suitable answer to a trouble. In case you need help with divergent thinking (finding a couple of answers to a trouble), carrying out more improvised kinds of dance along with hip-hop or tap might simply do the trick.

2. workout Your mind with logic Puzzles or games

The prevailing method whilst gambling chess, Sudoku, a Rubik's cube, or other brain-boosting games is surely to paintings the trouble backward, no longer forward. The identical method can observe to sensible strategic-thinking situations to build up your brain muscle and develop new problem-solving techniques, exercise a few common sense puzzles and different games.

3. Get a very good night's Sleep

extra than some other sound asleep or awake country, speedy Eye movement (REM) sleep immediately complements creative processing inside the mind. REM sleep enables "stimulate associative networks, allowing the brain to make new and beneficial institutions between unrelated ideas" and are "no longer due to selective reminiscence enhancements" which includes reminiscence consolidation, which happens when wide awake.

4. Exercise session to some Tunes

A study of cardiac rehabilitation sufferers tested verbal fluency after exercising with and without music. results showed that once they listened to music while operating out, contributors greater than doubled their ratings on verbal fluency checks in assessment to when they labored out in silence. According to the have a look at's lead writer, "The combination of track and exercising might also stimulate and increase cognitive arousal while assisting to organize the cognitive output."

5. Preserve a "concept magazine" with you

Trouble solving with a journal you'll be capable of fast file vital mind, write down personal reports, make sketches, and discover ideas when you hold a "concept journal" with you always. Working out issues by sorting your mind on paper and then viewing them more objectively is less difficult than having all your thoughts caught in your head (and will provide better hassle-solving strategies).

6. Take part in Yoga

The effective mixture of frame recognition, respiratory, and meditation that is required throughout yoga practice has been shown to noticeably raise cognitive check rankings. Other effects from a university of Illinois observe include shorter response instances, greater accuracy, and accelerated interest.

7. eat a few Cheerios (and then consider It)

The Cheerios impact is the call physicists have given to the occasion that occurs while the previous few cheerios in a bowl constantly dangle to each other . The reason of this occurrence is surface tension. The takeaway is that on the subject of experiencing tension while trying to resolve a problem, hold to those around you. Rely on others' stories and ideas, even those from different career fields. Draw connections. Brainstorm. Paintings collectively to get the process finished.

8. Use thoughts Maps to help Visualize the problem

thoughts Maps, a visible snapshot of a trouble and its feasible answers, can help attention the thoughts, stimulate the mind, boom the potential for creative wondering, and generate extra ideas for answers. Make a thoughts Map by means of drawing your hassle because the significant concept. upload "important branches" including all of the reasons for the problem. Use "sub-branches" to explore similarly info. Next, make a separate mind Map of all feasible answers to the significant problem. Upload "primary branches" showing all of the ways that your problem may be solved, which includes colleagues that can help, strategies you may observe, and other assets you can use. Add "sub-branches" to in addition discover the info. Make a very last branch with the most suitable answer for the primary problem. Use "sub-branches" for information.

Via this exercise, you should be able to see which "branch" or option is the maximum realistic, time-saving, and price-effective trouble solving approach.

Fundamental regulations problem solving

the entirety on this listing is considered a must and if you are extreme approximately constructing skills around problem fixing in yourself and in your employer, they ought to be non-negotiable.

1) Are seeking for, absorb, and recognize all the critical sources of information in your environment

We stay in an age if endless information. Every person in a business surroundings should scan their enterprise environment through the records amassing from reliable and applicable resources of facts. This consists of widespread information, enterprise news, enterprise information, and virtual resources which includes agencies, and experts.

2) Aggressive preparation

"Winging it" is simply no longer proper. Problem fixing starts off evolved with aggressive guidance this means that considering questioning and ensuring opportunities are blanketed and all sources of information had been used appropriately to put together for an afternoon, week, month, 12 months, and all activities.

3). Plan your day and make sensible to-do lists

competitive coaching is the inspiration for executing plans thru proactive planning and to-do lists which might be sensible. By way of proactively making plans and being on top of things of information and conditions, the point of interest can be at the duties to hand which have to be the matters necessary to execute the business approach.

4). Don't simply be on time, be early

showing up simply while the day is beginning or whilst conferences are starting isn't proactive and doesn't assist critical wondering and trouble solving; it in all likelihood makes matters worse. Being 15 mins early lets in for the capacity to look matters that others don't see (or hear) and that records can be used as part of the journey.

5) Be gift, listen, and research

to start with, positioned the phone AWAY! Put it on your pocket. Unless you are in a vital position like income or customer service wherein the execution of your method is based on your instant reaction, put it AWAY. Be present and consciousness. Nobody can assume significantly if half of their attention is on a leaderboard on buzz feed. It's ridiculous. After you positioned your phone away, then concentrate and learn. Every experience, every new piece of expertise builds the ability resolv e problems of the business.

6) Proportion insights (but don't blather)

Human beings suppose critically and resolve problems are able to really percentage their insights without talking an excessive amount of, over-selling, or blathering on approximately non-experience. By using surely sharing insights, you are then capable of listen to reactions and quality -music your procedures.

7) Well known whilst you don't realize something

Even the first-rate critical thinkers don't know the whole lot; but they do have a manner for figuring matters out. Acknowledge while you don't understand something and proactively are looking for the proper facts through the right resources.

8) Be respectful inside the system

No person likes a smartass-recognize-it-all. The first-rate important thinkers are respectful and construct assets even though humility and gratitude. They build a portfolio of expertise and acquire methods and techniques of trouble solving that depend upon other people nine) Don't cut corners

One of the maximum important factors of top, robust problem solving is doing it right and now not reducing any corners. Slicing corners will unavoidably come up with the incorrect solution and a poor business result.

10) Take pleasure in your work

And sooner or later, the maximum important rule; take monstrous pleasure and possession to your work. With the aid of searching for to be the great at what you do and searching for to be the excellent to your enterprise, you'll effortlessly discover the right paths alongside the adventure. Pride is that the most essential ingredient in vital speculative and problem finding as a result of it implicitly drives you to work things move into ways in which you didn't suppose were antecedently viable

Critical Thinking

The Fundamental and Concise Guide to
Master Smart Decision Making,
Intelligent Reasoning, Negotiating, Deep
and Quick Analysis, and Independent
Thinking Like Never Before
Part-2

BY

Henry Fennimore

Critical Thinking

acknowledge that the author is not engaging in the rendering of legal, financial, medical or professional advice. The content within this book has been derived from various sources. Please consult a licensed professional before attempting any techniques outlined in this book.

By reading this document, the reader agrees that under no circumstances is the author responsible for any losses, direct or indirect, which are incurred as a result of the use of information contained within this document, including, but not limited to, — errors, omissions, or inaccuracies.

Description

One of a kind in context, this book gives a general way to deal with basic reasoning aptitudes that can be applied to all controls. With an accentuation on composing, just as on choosing what to accept or do, it offers broadened dialogs, models, and practice of such abilities as watching, making decisions, arranging investigations, and creating thoughts and choices.

Characterizes the structure and substance of the basic deduction course, at schools and colleges the nation over. This incorporates the ideas of basic intuition, with models significant to understudies.

Business associations are in consistent and quickening emergency. This reality is clear to such an extent that we quit monitoring it completely and we concentrate on specific regions rather, attempting to address them in segregation. Likewise, while tending to huge issues influencing business, we look for arrangements and - which is far more terrible point of view inside the business space itself: we go to directors, experts and scholastics spend significant time in different parts of business. This nearsighted mindset has discovered its way to the bigger space of financial aspects and governmental issues which are being run as organizations, further strengthening the overall emergency.

Our reason is straightforward: to take care of our issues or to trigger positive change we have to look outside of the business area, even outside of the cutting edge attitude that brought forth business in any case, go past transient speculations, reach back to the basics, draw on immortal shrewdness and discover approaches to apply them in the present setting.

While the book seeks after an interdisciplinary way to deal with basic reasoning, giving models and outlines from various subjects and fields of research, it likewise gives methodologies to assist perusers with distinguishing the strategies and benchmarks that are normal for basic intuition in their picked parts of learning, in their working environment, and in their own lives. The idea of a contention is reached out past its philosophical roots to incorporate experimentation, testing, estimation, approach advancement and evaluation, and stylish gratefulness as exercises that require basic reasoning. The legitimate, center ideas of basic reasoning are introduced in a thorough yet casual manner, with inventive and down to earth methodologies for characterizing, dissecting, and assessing reasons and contentions any place they are found.

History

John Dewey (1910: seventy four, eighty two) brought the term 'significant addressing' as the name of a scholastic expectation, which he perceived with an efficient attitude of considerations. Extra ordinarily, he called the objective 'intelligent thought', 'intelligent reasoning', 'reflection', or basically 'thought' or 'thinking'. He depicts his book as composed for 2 capacities. The first was to help people to understand the family relationship of adolescents' neighborhood interest, ripe innovativeness and love of trial request to the therapeutic frame of mind. The subsequent one changed into to help individuals to remember how detecting this family relationship in instructional practice "could make for man or lady satisfaction and the decrease of social waste" (iii). He noticed that the considerations in the digital book got solidness in the Laboratory staff in Chicago.

Dewey's considerations have been put into training by means of some of the schools that took an interest inside the 8-year look at in the Nineteen Thirties sponsored by utilizing the cutting edge instruction connection in the America. For this examine, 300 schools consented to remember for affirmation alumni of 30 settled on auxiliary resources or school structures from over the U.S. A. who tried different things with the substance and strategies of instructing, regardless of whether the alumni had now not completed the then-recommended auxiliary school educational program. One reason for the examination changed into to discover through investigation and experimentation how auxiliary schools inside the usa should serve youths all the more accurately.Each trial school transformed into free to trade the educational program as it saw coordinate, anyway the universities concurred that instructing procedures and the presence of the school need to follow the idea (recently supported by Dewey) that people grow by means of doing things which can be huge to them, and that the fundamental rationale of the optional school was to control youthful individuals to comprehend, acknowledge and remain the popularity based way of life highlight of the usa. Especially, school authorities accepted that youthful people in a majority rule government need to build up the dependancy of intelligent reasoning and ability in taking care of issues. undergrads' work inside the examination space therefore comprised extra as often as possible of an issue to be comprehended than an exercise to be educated. primarily in math and innovation, the resources tried giving understudies revel in clear, legitimate addressing as they tackled issues. The report of 1 trial workforce, the college school of Ohio state school, explained this point of upgrading understudies' pondering:

Imperative or intelligent addressing starts with the detecting of an issue. it is a high-caliber of idea working with the goal that you can clear up the issue and to accomplish a speculative end that is bolstered by all to be had records. it's far in actuality a strategy for issue fixing requiring the utilization of inventive discernment, highbrow genuineness, and sound judgment. it's far the premise of the strategy for clinical request. The satisfaction of vote based system depends to an enormous degree at the attitude and capacity of occupants to expect harshly and brilliantly roughly the difficulties which need to of need go up against them, and to improve the best of their scrutinizing is one of the fundamental fantasies about tutoring. (Commission on the Relation of staff and school of the advanced preparing association.

The 8-year watch had an evaluation staff, which created, in discussion with the schools, appraisals to degree components of understudy progress that fell outside the point of convergence of the customary educational program. The appraisal group of laborers named a great deal of the resources' said focuses under the ordinary heading "unwavering discernment" or "significant reasoning". To create checks of accomplishment of this immense objective, they recognized five covering parts of it: capacity to translate measurements, abilities related with an expertise of the character of proof, and the abilities to apply ideas of science, of social research and of consistent thinking. The 8-year watch moreover had a school gathering of laborers, coordinated by a board of trustees of college overseers, whose task changed into to decide how pleasantly the trial schools had arranged their alumni for school. The school work force as looked at the general execution of 1,475 undergrads from the trial resources with an indistinguishable wide assortment of graduates from conventional universities, coordinated two by two with the guide of intercourse, age, race, educational energy evaluations, home and system verifiable past, leisure activities, and potentially fate. They presumed that, on 18 proportions of understudy accomplishment, the alumni of the exploratory schools did a moderately higher procedure than the evaluation establishment. The alumni from the six generally regular of the trial schools affirmed no gigantic or relentless varieties. The alumni from the six most test resources, then again, had an extraordinary arrangement additional varieties in support of them. The alumni of the two greatest trial resources, the college group of laborers stated:

Outperformed their examination organizations with the guide of colossal edges in scholarly achievement, scholarly interest, therapeutic way to deal with inconveniences, and enthusiasm for present day undertakings. The distinctions of their pick have been considerably more prominent in standard cleverness, in diversion of dissecting, [in] investment in expressions of the human experience, in triumphing non-instructive distinctions, and in all elements of college presence with the exception of more then likely interest in sports exercises and social exercises. This sort of resources turned into an individual school with understudies from advantaged family units and the option the trial segment of an open staff with undergrads from non-favored families. The school group of laborers said that the alumni of the 2 schools had been undefined from each other regarding college accomplishment.

In 1933 Dewey gave an obviously revamped rendition of his How We accept , with the sub-name "A rehashing of the connection of intelligent addressing to the educative system". In spite of the way that the repetition keeps the essential structure and substance of the first digital book, Dewey made some of alterations. He revamped and streamlined his consistent examination of the strategy for reflected picture, made his considerations more clear and increasingly specific, changed the expressions 'enlistment' and 'conclusion' by methods for the expressions 'control of data and verification' and 'oversee of thinking and thoughts', brought more noteworthy representations, reworked sections, and reconsidered the parts on instructing to reflect alterations in schools since 1910. exceptionally, he questioned 1 -sided practices of a couple "exploratory" and "present day" resources that permitted youths opportunity anyway gave them no steerage, raising as shocking practices oddity and assortment for the good of their own one of a kind, stories and sports with genuine materials anyway of no instructional significance, regarding arbitrary and separated diversion just as it were a trial, inability to abridge web achievement on the quit of a request, non-educative activities, and cure of the coach as an immaterial angle in inclination to as "the highbrow chief of a social association". with out clarifying his reasons, Dewey disposed of the first version's utilizes of the expressions 'significant' and 'uncritical', therefore settling solidly on 'reflected picture' or 'intelligent reasoning' on the grounds that the ideal term for his test depend. inside the amended release, the word 'pivotal' happens best once, in which Dewey composes that "an individual may not be adequately indispensable about the thoughts that emerge to him" ; being critical is as an outcome an issue of reflection, no longer its total. In assessment, the 8-yr see by the progressive preparing affiliation managed 'crucial addressing' and 'intelligent intuition' as equivalent words.

inside a similar length, Dewey worked together on a records of the Laboratory school in Chicago with previous educators from the school . The records portrays the school's educational program and association, sports designed for developing abilties, mother and father' inclusion, and the direct of mind that the kids gained. A finishing up chapter 11 assesses the school's accomplishments, considering a triumph its arranging of the educational program to relate to the regular improvement of the developing infant. In two supplements, the creators depict the advancement of Dewey's ideas of instruction and Dewey himself portrays the possibility of the Chicago try .

Glaser (1941) audits in his doctoral paper the technique and aftereffects of a test in the improvement of significant addressing directed in the fall of 1938. He characterizes fundamental addressing as Dewey depicted intelligent pondering:

Basic reasoning requires an industrious endeavor to take a gander at any conviction or expected state of ability inside the gentle of the evidence that supports it and the likewise ends to which it tends. In the test, 8 exercise devices coordinated at improving significant addressing aptitudes were educated to four evaluation 12 unreasonable workforce classes, with pre-check and distribute check of the researchers the utilization of the Otis brief-Scoring scholarly capacity test and the Watson-Glaser appraisals of critical addressing (created as a team with Glaser's exposition support, Goodwin Watson). The normal advantage in scores on those checks become more noteworthy to a measurably decent estimated degree a portion of the understudies who get:

The part of basic pondering which appears to be greatest inclined to broad improvement is the outlook of being arranged to remember in a mindful way the issues and subjects that come inside the assortment of 1's revel in. An outlook of needing proof for standards is additional worry to stylish exchange. improvement of expertise in applying the strategies for consistent request and thinking, yet, is by all accounts specifically identified with, and in reality limited by methods for, the acquisition of relevant comprehension and certainties in regards to the difficulty or concern depend towards which the believing is to be coordinated.

Retest rankings and detectable conduct showed that understudies in the intercession association held their blast in capacity to expect altogether for at any rate a half year after the interesting direction. In 1948 an assortment of U.S. school analysts chose to expand scientific classifications of instructional exercise focuses with an ordinary jargon that they may use for talking with each other about investigate things. the first of those scientific classifications, for the subjective area, showed up in 1956 and included crucial addressing targets. It has come to be called Bloom's scientific classification. A subsequent scientific classification, for the full of feeling area, and a third scientific categorization, for the psychomotor space respected later. everything about scientific categorizations is various leveled, with accomplishment of a superior instructive goal claimed to require accomplishment of comparing decline scholarly destinations.

Blossom's scientific categorization has six fundamental classes. From most minimal to most elevated, they're data, understanding, programming, assessment, blend, and assessment. Inside each class, there are sub-classes, likewise sorted out progressively from the instructively preceding the instructively back. The base class, however called 'data', is restricted to destinations of recollecting records and having the option to remember or get it, absent a lot of change past sorting out it The five better classes are as one named "scholarly capabilities and capacities" The term is without a doubt some other call for significant pondering aptitudes and abilities:

Notwithstanding the way that data or comprehension is distinguished as an essential result of tutoring, not many educators could be fulfilled to regard this as the essential or the sole result of training. What is required is some proof that the researchers can do something with their skill, that will be, that they could pursue the measurements to new conditions and inconveniences. It is additionally foreseen that researchers will get summed up strategies for dealing with new inconveniences and new materials.

Therefore, it's miles expected that after the researcher experiences a shiny new issue or circumstance, he will pick the exact strategy for assaulting it and will bring to experience the significant records, every record and thoughts. This has been marked "basic pondering" by method for a few, "intelligent reasoning" through Dewey and others, and "critical thinking" by means of by and by others. In the scientific classification, we have utilized the expression "highbrow capacities and gifts".

Perception and sharpness objectives, as their names propose, include ability and utilizing information. Basic reasoning aptitudes and abilities show up inside the three most extreme classes of assessment, combination and assessment. The consolidated variant of Bloom's scientific categorization gives the resulting instances of destinations at those levels:

Assessment objectives: potential to comprehend implicit suspicions, potential to test the consistency of speculations with given records and presumptions, capacity to perceive the general techniques used in promoting, publicity and distinctive enticing substances

Union goals: arranging thoughts and proclamations recorded as a hard copy, potential to advocate methods for looking at a speculation, potential to detail and direct theories.

Assessment targets: capacity to recommend sensible paradoxes, complexity of head hypotheses about explicit societies.

The assessment, combination and appraisal focuses in Bloom's scientific classification all in all came to be known as the "better-request pondering abilities". In spite of the fact that the assessment combination appraisal assortment emulates arranges in Dewey's (1933) sensible examination of the intelligent reasoning procedure, it has not normally been embraced as a model of an essential pondering framework. Simultaneously as complimenting the helpful cost of its proportion of 5 classes of addressing objectives to in any event one classification of think about targets, Ennis (1981b) factors out that the sorts need criteria important all through subjects and area names. for instance, assessment in science is so not quite the same as investigation in writing that there isn't in every case bounty point in showing assessment as well known kind of reasoning. So also, the proposed pecking order seems faulty on the higher phases of Bloom's scientific classification. For instance, ability to recommend intelligent paradoxes barely shows up extra muddled than the capacity to compose proclamations and musings recorded as a hard copy.

A modified rendition of Bloom's scientific classification recognizes the alleged subjective framework in an instructive objective (comprehensive of being equipped for consider, to contrast or with test) from the objective's educational substance ("information"), which can be genuine, applied, procedural, or metacognitive. The outcome is a so-known as "Scientific categorization table" with 4 lines for the styles of educational substance material and six segments for the six chief types of subjective system. The creators call the kinds of subjective way through action words, to recommend their status as scholarly sports. They trade the call of the 'appreciation' class to 'perceive' and of the 'blend' classification to 'make', and switch the request for amalgamation and assessment. The outcome is a posting of six most significant sorts of subjective strategy pointed toward with the guide of instructors: remember, secure, watch, look at, assess, and make. The creators keep the possibility of a chain of command of expanding unpredictability, however understood some cover, for instance among comprehension and applying. What's more, that they hold the idea that basic pondering and bother explaining diminish all through the additional complex intellectual techniques. The expressions 'basic pondering' and 'issue fixing', they compose:

Are comprehensively utilized and by and large will in general rise as touchstones of educational program accentuation. Each by and large comprise of a determination of exercises that is most likely sorted in different cells of the Taxonomy table. This is, in some random model, focuses on that include critical thinking and significant reasoning most extreme likely call for psychological strategies in a few classifications at the procedure measurement. As a case, to think seriously around a difficulty likely involves some Conceptual mastery to look into the trouble. At that point, you'll have the option to assess unmistakable perspectives as far as the criteria and, perhaps, Create an interesting, yet faultless frame of mind in this issue.

Inside the changed scientific categorization, just some sub-classes, for example, inducing, have enough shared trait to be treated as an awesome imperative reasoning capacity that would ponder and evaluated as an in vogue limit. A milestone commitment to philosophical grant at the idea of basic reasoning become a A proposed reason for contemplates in the educating and appraisal of significant addressing potential" Ennis took as his starting element a thought of essential pondering set forward with the guide of B. Othanel Smith:

We will thought in expressions of the tasks worried inside the test of proclamations which we, or others, may concur with. A speaker declares, for instance, that "Opportunity strategy that the decisions in the US's proficient exertion are made now not inside the brains of an administration anyway in the free commercial center". Presently in the event that we set roughly to discover what this announcement way and to choose whether to simply acknowledge or dismiss it, we'd be occupied with intuition which, for absence of a superior timeframe, we will call basic pondering. On the off chance that one wants to state that that is best a state of issue fixing in which the explanation is to choose whether or not or now not what's said is trustworthy, we won't thing. be that as it may, for our capacities we choose to call it vital pondering.

Adding a regulating issue to this idea, Ennis characterized urgent addressing as "the exact evaluating of proclamations" On the reason of this definition, he remarkable 12 "components" of critical pondering like sorts or components of explanations, which incorporate making a decision about whether a perception revelation is solid and getting a handle on the significance of a presentation. He alluded to that he did never again incorporate making a decision about worth articulations. straightforward over the 12 viewpoints, he exceptional three elements of basic addressing: legitimate (making a decision about connections among implications of expressions and proclamations), criterial (know-how of the criteria for passing judgment on explanations), and down to business (the impression of the foundation intention). For every perspective, Ennis depicted the appropriate measurements, including criteria. He proposed the subsequent amass as an establishment for creating specs for basic addressing checks and for thinks about on scholarly methodologies and levels.

In the Nineteen Seventies and Eighties there was an upsurge important to the improvement of pondering abilities. the yearly worldwide gathering on significant pondering and scholarly Reform has pulled in since its beginning in 1980 a huge number of instructors.

Critical Thinking

Introduction

Basic reasoning is independently directed, self-trained reasoning which endeavors to reason at the most significant level of value in an honest manner. Individuals who think basically reliably endeavor to live objectively, sensibly, empathically. They are distinctly mindful of the characteristically defective nature of human reasoning when left unchecked. They endeavor to reduce the intensity of their egocentric and sociocentric inclinations. They utilize the scholarly devices that basic reasoning offers – ideas and rules that empower them to break down, survey, and improve thinking. They work steadily to build up the scholarly temperance's of scholarly uprightness, scholarly modesty, scholarly consideration, scholarly sympathy, scholarly feeling of equity and trust in reason. They understand that regardless of how talented they are as scholars, they can generally improve their thinking capacities and they will on occasion fall prey to botches in thinking, human unreasonableness, preferences, predispositions, mutilations, uncritically acknowledged social standards and taboos, personal circumstance, and personal stake. They endeavor to improve the world in the manners they can and add to an increasingly reasonable, enlightened society. Simultaneously, they perceive the complexities frequently inborn in doing as such. They abstain from contemplating entangled issues and endeavor to fittingly think about the rights and needs of significant others. They perceive the complexities in creating as scholars, and invest in long lasting practice toward personal growth. They encapsulate the Socratic standard: The unexamined life does not merit living, in light of the fact that they understand that numerous unexamined lives respectively bring about an uncritical, low, risky world.

Essential thinking is that the examination of assurances to frame a judgment. The subject is exceptional, and some particular definitions exist, that for the chief half fuse the fair, far-fetched, unprejudiced assessment, or evaluation of right confirmation. Essential thinking is independently directed, self-prepared, self-watched, and self-healing thinking. It expect agree to intensive checks of enormity and cautious course of their usage. It includes ground-breaking correspondence and requesting thinking limits even as and assurance to beat local egotism and sociocentrism.

Hypothetical Domain

Hypothetical basic reasoning includes helping the understudy build up a thankfulness for logical clarifications of conduct. This implies learning the substance of brain science as well as how and why brain research is sorted out into ideas, standards, laws, and speculations. Creating hypothetical aptitudes starts in the early on course where the essential basic reasoning goal is understanding and applying ideas suitably. For instance, when you acquaint understudies with the standards of fortification, you can solicit them to discover models from the standards in the news or to make up stories that show the standards.

Mid-level courses in the major require more complexity, moving understudies past use of ideas and standards to learning and applying hypotheses. For example, you can give a rich contextual analysis in irregular brain research and solicit understudies to bode well from the case from alternate points of view, underlining hy pothetical adaptability or precise utilization of existing and acknowledged systems in brain science to clarify examples of conduct. In cutting edge courses we can reasonably request that understudies assess hypothesis, choosing the most valuable or dismissing the least supportive. For instance, understudies can differentiate various models to clarify illicit drug use in physiological brain science. By looking at the qualities and shortcomings of existing systems, they can choose which hypotheses serve best as they figure out how to legitimize their reactions dependent on proof and reason.

Capstone, praises, and graduate courses go past hypothesis assessment to urge understudies to make hypothesis. Understudies select an intricate inquiry concerning conduct (for instance, recognizing instruments that underlie chemical imbalance or language procurement) and build up their own hypothesis based clarifications for the conduct. This test expects them to orchestrate and coordinate existing hypothesis just as devise new bits of knowledge into the conduct.

Present brain research as an open-finished, developing endeavor. Understudies regularly imagine that their entrance into the control speaks to an end-point where everything great and genuine has just been found. That end supports lack of involvement instead of criticality. Point out that examination is brain science' s method for developing and creating. Each new disclosure in brain research speaks to a conceivably rich demonstration of basic reasoning. A ton of space for disclosure remains. New thoughts will be created and old originations disposed of.Require understudy execution that goes past remembrance. Gathering work, expositions, discusses, subjects, letters to well known therapists, diaries, recent development models these and more can be utilized as a methods for building up the higher abilities associated with basic speculation in brain science. Find broken reason impact ends in the sensationalist newspapers. Solicit understudies to recognize what sorts from proof would warrant faith in business claims. In spite of the fact that it is troublesome, even all around structured target test things can catch basic reasoning aptitudes with the goal that understudies are tested past insignificant reiteration and review.

Explain your assumptions regarding execution with express, open criteria. Formulating clear execution criteria for brain science activities will upgrade understudy achievement. Understudies frequently grumble that they don't comprehend "what you need" when you appoint work. Execution criteria determine the gauges that you will use to assess their work. For instance, perfonnance criteria for the perception practice depicted before might incorporate the accompanying: The understudy portrays conduct precisely; offers derivation that is sensible for the specific circumstance; and recognizes individual factors that may impact deduction. Perfonnance criteria encourage giving itemized criticism effectively and can likewise advance understudy self-evaluation.

Support a scrutinizing mentality. Understudies regularly accept that on the off chance that they have inquiries regarding their perusing, at that point they are some way or another being shameful, inconsiderate, or dumb. Having dialogs right off the bat in the course about the job of good inquiries in upgrading the nature of the subject and extending the sharpness of the brain may set a progressively basic stage on which understudies can play. Model basic speculation from certain bits of knowledge you have had about conduct or from some examination you have directed previously. Compliment understudies who offer genuine instances of the standards under investigation. Thank understudies who ask idea related inquiries and portray for what good reason you think their inquiries are great. Leave existence for additional. Your own energy about basic reasoning can be an extraordinary motivator for understudies to look for that fervor.

Basic Thinking in Everyday Life

Have you at any point been tuning in to one of your educator's exercises and felt that it had no significance to your own life? You're not the only one. Pretty much every understudy has felt a similar way. Without a doubt, you utilize basic speculation abilities in the homeroom to take care of word issues in math, compose papers in English, and make theories in science.

Be that as it may, by what method will you utilize basic speculation in regular day to day existence? To start with, remember that basic reasoning is essentially an "intentional manner of thinking."

Fundamentally, it implies that you are utilizing reason and rationale to reach a decision about an issue or choice you are going head to head with. What's more, clear, stable thinking is something that will help you consistently. To assist you with making the jump from study hall to genuine world, here are 3 solid instances of basic intuition in regular day to day existence.

Counterfeit News versus Genuine News

Pause for a minute to think about your media aptitudes. Do you think you have the stuff to sift through a genuine news source from a bit of cunning promoting? As indicated by an ongoing report from Stanford University, an astounding 82% of the teenagers overviewed couldn't recognize a promotion named "supported substance" and a real news story.

Some portion of the issue may return from schools cutting on formal guidance of basic reasoning aptitudes and a suspicion that the present "advanced local" youngsters can naturally differentiate without training or guidance. You are great at bunches of things. Be that as it may, you know, you've drilled those things you're great at. All in all, how might you work on telling actuality from fiction?

One way (outside of school) is to talk with your loved ones about media sources. Discover how they remain educated, and why they pick those outlets. Approach each other routine inquiries for assessing sources.

Do your Friends Know Everything?

It's enticing to accept that the world starts and finishes with your companions. Try not to misunderstand me. Companions are certainly significant. Be that as it may, it pays to mirror a little on how a gathering impacts our lives.

To rehearse basic deduction in regular day to day existence, investigate your gathering of companions. Are there things that are "prohibited" in your group of friends? It is safe to say that you are required to act a specific way, dress a specific way?

Think a specific way?

It's characteristic that when a gathering characterizes something as "cool", every one of the individuals in the gathering work to fit into that definition. Notwithstanding what they separately accept. The issue is that for all intents and purposes each circumstance can be characterized in numerous manners. What is "stupidity" to one individual can be "fine" to another. Build up your capacity to rethink the manner in which you see your general surroundings. All alone terms.

Discover when your companion bunch sees the negative in a circumstance. Is there a positive method to see it? Or if nothing else a way that causes it to appear not exactly so awful? You may not be prepared to make some noise with your autonomous view. What's more, that is alright. Simply work on deduction uniquely in contrast to the gathering to fortify your psyche.

Basic Thinking in the Driver's Seat

One of the center basic reasoning aptitudes you need each day is the capacity to look at the suggestions and results of a conviction or activity. In its most profound structure, this capacity can assist you with shaping your very own arrangement of convictions in everything from environmental change to religion. Be that as it may, this aptitude can likewise spare your life (and your vehicle protection rate) in the driver's seat.

Envision you are cruising down the interstate when your telephone cautions you to an approaching instant message. The capacity to look at your latent capacity activities and their going with outcomes will assist you with settling on the best decision for how to deal with the circumstance.

Do you take a gander at the content and hazard getting into a mishap? Do you pause and hazard not reacting to a pressing issue? Or on the other hand do you destroy over to take a gander at the content and hazard being late for your arrangement? A similar expertise can be applied when you are searching for a spot to stop, when to pull onto a bustling road, or whether to run the yellow light. Even better, the more rehearsed you are at taking a gander at the ramifications of your driving propensities, the quicker you can settle on split second choices in the driver's seat.

Why crucial Thinking in lifestyle Matters

Actually everyone will profit by basic reasoning in lightweight of the very fact that the necessity for its close US. In a philosophical paper, Peter Facione puts forth a solid defense that basic reasoning aptitudes are needed by everyone, altogether social orders United Nations agency esteem well-being, equity, and an oversized cluster of alternative positive qualities:

"Considered as a sort of perceptive judgment or intelligent basic leadership, undeniably basic reasoning is ineluctable. There's not very an amount or a spot wherever it'd not seem to be of potential value. For no matter length of your time that people have functions at the highest of the priority list and need to pass judgment on the foremost skilled methodology to realize them, to that degree as people surprise what's valid and what is not, what to just accept and what to dismiss, solid basic reasoning are going to be basic." Along these lines, as such, as long as you keep inquisitive, deliberate, and goal-oriented, in spite of what your inclinations, you are going to need basic intuition to really possess your life.

Why essential Thinking Matters in Your Business

It is the desire for specialists to chase when occupations they're vivacious in regards to. Though finding indescribable paradise and importance from one's work is useful for benefit, it's basic to ensure extraordinary sentiments and main impetuses don't cloud fundamental instinct inside the working environment. Experts should use essential hypothesis by and large segments of working surroundings exercises to deal with a vital good ways from extortionate mistakes. From enlistment to displaying and arrangements, each definitive division needs to underline practicing fundamental hypothesis in work surroundings choices.

Jen Lawrence, co-maker of have collaboration the Fox: A Business Fable in regards to Thinking Critically and Motivating Your Team, portrays fundamental hypothesis as "the capacity to require care of issues feasibly by intentionally gathering data in regards to a trouble, fabricating more musings together with Associate in Nursing combination of purposes of read, surveying the information using clarification, and ensuring everybody identified with arranged."

This is a stunning definition for a perplexing arrangement. In spite of the undeniable reality that it will appear as simple as wandering back and using a standard hypothesis strategy as basic reacting naturally to conflicts or issues, this can be harder than one would conceivably anticipate. Fundamental thinking abilities will and should be instructed inside the work environment so they become normal. Essential thinking is significant in light-weight of the established truth that it ensures you have the best reaction to a trouble, with most outrageous buy in from all social occasions encased – an outcome which can in the end save your business time, cash and stress. Here's the style by that to handle, grasp and realize fundamental instinct in your working environment.

Showing basic deduction in the work environment

David Welton, overseeing accomplice at Grove Critical Thinking, says basic reasoning is "an open to instruction expertise." He takes note of that basic reasoning is regularly miscategorized as a delicate ability, however delicate aptitudes are not assertive. On the off chance that businesses and workers the same don't think basic reasoning is assertive, it is simple for it to be left by the wayside.

Both Lawrence and Welton suggest investigating basic reasoning trainings and strategies to improve your work environment's general basic reasoning capability. Those in official and administrative positions can start with an evaluation of which regions of the work environment appear to be generally ailing in basic reasoning.

In the event that mix-ups are reliably being made, it is useful to initially investigate whether the issue is an absence of basic reasoning, not an intrinsic issue with a representative or gathering of workers. At that point, you can examine what trainings, mentors or educational plans may accommodate your association best begin rehearsing straightforward hypothesis as a predilection with littler issues as fashions, and in a while stir your manner up to larger troubles," Lawrence aforementioned. Basic reasoning is tied in with tackling issues through discerning procedures and proof based information. Like the logical technique, basic reasoning contains a ton of steps, as Lawrence noted in her definition, yet these means will spare a great deal of time over the long haul if missteps can be forestalled.

Moving toward issues with a free, intelligent manner of thinking is one sort of basic reasoning. Basic reasoning structures contentions from proof, while naming issues and suspicions that can hinder assessing an issue for what it is. It's tied in with taking care of issues in a procedure focused way that benefits from information and target proof – and in the business world, these abilities set aside time and cash start to finish. Not exclusively will it spare your business expensive assets, yet basic reasoning will likewise improve other working environment abilities, for example, correspondence, imagination, logical competency, enthusiastic knowledge and general critical thinking.

Setting aside time and cash with basic reasoning

24-hour sequence of media reports and flood of unchecked certainties over -burdens our minds all through the working environment. Lawrence said this adds to a hysterical working environment rhythm that fortifies hurried reasoning and business choices. This is when expensive mix-ups and bumbles are made.

Welton included that basic reasoning makes people better scholars, yet better communicators. Within the occasion that you simply will think all of the additional signally and higher fluent your positions, you'll be able to all the extra likely connect with talks and construct a notably additional vital dedication in your pastime." It may appear to be nonsensical to connect expository levelheadedness with passionate, significant commitment, yet when you can feel certain and careful in your basic leadership process, the final product will feel additionally satisfying and yield enthusiastic insight.

Much the same as basic reasoning procedures themselves, instructing and executing basic reasoning preparing and philosophy requires some investment and tolerance. Lawrence underlined that basic reasoning abilities are best procured in a period of quiet. It may feel earnest to search out basic speculation during an emergency, yet it is a hard aptitude to learn in a frenzy. Basic reasoning preparing is best done preemptively – that way, when an emergency hits, representatives will be readied and basic reasoning will work out easily.

From an official or administrative point of view, giving workers additional time on ventures or tackling issues may feel like a stressor if there are cutoff times or weights from higher up. Yet, in the event that you need those working for you to take part in basic reasoning procedures, it's basic to give them an opportunity to do as such. Once more, a portion of the pressure can be maintained a strategic distance from if basic reasoning is instructed preemptively, not if all else fails. Giving workers this additional time will really spare the organization time and cash over the long haul.

Distinguishing effective basic reasoning

Showing representatives basic deduction in the working environment enables them to utilize the expertise as an emergency occurs, not sometime later. Lawrence gave a model including eateries and waitstaff: If a client has an awful involvement with an eatery, a server utilizing basic reasoning aptitudes will be bound to make sense of an answer for spare the association, for example, offering a free canapé or rebate. "This could spare the nicely-deserved client qualitative analysis you spent a unbelievable deal of showcasing greenbacks to form."

This idea is appropriate crosswise over numerous business and hierarchical structures. While the café model passes on basic reasoning abilities, you ought to likewise know about the indications of an absence of those aptitudes. Organizations that change system quickly, moving starting with one thing then onto the next, are likely not participating in basic reasoning, said Lawrence. This is additionally the situation in organizations that appear to experience smart thoughts however experience issues executing them.

Likewise with numerous issues in business, what's going on at the top is a decent signifier of how present basic believing is in the remainder of the association. On the off chance that an organization has a shrewd pioneer with good thoughts yet no procedures being pursued, there will be no upfront investment, and the organization will endure. This is the reason basic reasoning abilities regularly go with positive relational abilities.

"Basic reasoning wouldn't while not a doubt assist you with landing at the high-quality answer, but at an answer a motivating several humans grasp," aforementioned Lawrence.Displaying basic intuition at the top will enable the ability to stream down to the remainder of the association, regardless of what kind or size of organization you have. At the point when missteps are kept away from and business is consistent at all levels, not exactly at the official level that implies basic reasoning is effectively executed in an association. Between trainings, time and persistence, basic reasoning can turn into a natural aptitude for representatives at all degrees of experience and position. The cash, time and strife you will spare over the long haul is certainly justified regardless of the additional time and persistence of actualizing basic intuition in your working environment.

The Skills we'd like for vital Thinking

The abilities that we'd like thus on have the choice to suppose basically square measure shifted and incorporate perception, investigation, elucidation, reflection, assessment, derivation, clarification, vital thinking, and basic leadership.

Explicitly we must always have the choice to:

Consider an issue or issue in an exceedingly target and basic manner.

- Recognize the varied contentions there square measure in association to a selected issue.

- Assess a degree of read to choose however solid or substantial it's.

- Perceive any shortcomings or negative focuses that there square measure within the proof or competition.

- Notice what suggestions there could also be behind Associate in Nursing announcement or competition.

- Give organized thinking and backing to a competition that we tend to want to create.

The important Thinking method

You got to understand that none people assume primarily perpetually. Some of the time we expect in much any manner nonetheless basically, as an example once our poise is influenced by outrage, pain or elation or once we area unit feeling out and out 'ridiculous disapproved'. Then again, as luck would have it, since our basic reasoning capability fluctuates as per our gift mentality, additional usually than not we will understand a way to improve our basic intuition capability by buildup sure commonplace exercises and applying them to all or any problems that gift themselves. When you comprehend the hypothesis of basic reasoning, up your basic reasoning aptitudes takes purpose and follow.

What are you progressing to Achieve?

One of the foremost vital components of basic basic cognitive process is to {settle onto decide on} what you're expecting to accomplish and later on settle on a selection addicted to a scope of conceivable outcomes.

When you have explained that specialize in yourself you must utilize it because the starting stage in each single future circumstance requiring thought and, perhaps, additional basic leadership. Wherever needed, build your coworkers, family or folks around you conscious of your goal to hunt once this objective. You must then teach yourself to stay heading in the right direction till dynamical conditions mean you wish to come back to the start of the fundamental leadership method.

In any case, there are things that hinder basic leadership. we have a tendency to as a full convey with North American nation a scope of various preferences, learnt practices and individual inclinations created for the length of our lives; they're the signs of being human. A big commitment to guaranteeing we predict primarily is to grasp concerning these individual attributes, inclinations and predispositions and provide leniency for them whereas brooding about conceivable resultant stages, notwithstanding whether or not they are at the pre-activity thought organize or as an element of a rethink caused by surprising or unexpected obstructions to proceed with progress.

The additional clearly we all know concerning ourselves, our qualities and shortcomings, the virtually sure our basic reasoning are going to be paid.

The Benefit of Foresight

Maybe the most significant component of reasoning basically is prescience. Practically all choices we make and actualize don't demonstrate sad on the off chance that we discover motivations to relinquish them. Notwithstanding, our basic leadership will be limitlessly better and bound to prompt achievement if, when we arrive at a speculative resolution, we stop and think about the effect on the individuals and exercises around us.

The components requiring thought are commonly various and shifted. As a rule, thought of one component from an alternate point of view will uncover potential perils in seeking after our choice.

For example, moving a business action to another area may improve potential yield extensively yet it might likewise prompt the loss of gifted laborers if the separation moved is excessively incredible. Which of these is the more significant thought? Is there some method for diminishing the contention? These are the kind of issues that may emerge from deficient basic reasoning, a showing maybe of the basic significance of good basic reasoning.

For what reason Do Employers worth vital Thinking Skills?

Bosses would like work up-and-comers United Nations agency will assess a circumstance utilizing legitimate plan and supply the simplest arrangement. Basic reasoning capacities area unit among the foremost searched for once talents in just about each business and dealing setting. You'll be able to show basic deduction by utilizing connected catchphrases in your resume and introductory letter, and through your meeting.

Instances of vital Thinking

The conditions that request basic intuition disagree from business to business. A couple of models include:

- A sorting nurture dissects the present cases and chooses the request by that the patients need to be forbidden.

- A fixer assesses the materials that might best suit a particular activity.

- An attorney audits proof and devises a procedure to win a case or to settle on whether or not to in camera address any remaining problems.

- A chief examines shopper criticism structures and uses this knowledge to create up a shopper care tutorial meeting for representatives.

Advance Your Skills in Your Job Search

On the off likelihood that essential thinking might be a key articulation inside the movement postings you're applying for, guarantee to underscore your fundamental instinct abilities at some phase in your quest for work.

Add Keywords to Your Resume

You can use fundamental thinking catchphrases (descriptive, basic reasoning, inventiveness, and afterward forward.) in your resume. While depiction your work history, consolidate any of the aptitudes recorded underneath that precisely delineate you. You'll have the option to in like manner remember them for your resume summation, on the off likelihood that you basically have one.

For example, your framework may analyze, "Publicizing go with 5 years of inclusion with adventure the board. Capable in directing cautious applied math mensuration and challenger assessment to gauge feature examples and customer needs, and to make right verifying ways."

Notice Skills in Your message

Recollect these essential theory aptitudes for you're early on letter. Inside the body of your letter, notice a bunch of those aptitudes, and gives express examples of times after you have demonstrated those abilities at work. Consider times after you required to analyze or evaluate materials to require care of a trouble.

Show the querier Your Skills

You can utilize these power words in an exceedingly meeting. Mention after you were looked with a selected issue or challenge at work and clarify however you applied basic speculation to know it.

A few questioners can offer you a speculative state of affairs or issue, and request that you simply utilize basic intuition skills to know it. For this case, clarify your perspective altogether to the verbalizer. The person is generally more and more targeted around however you land at your answer as hostile the arrangement itself. The verbalizer must see you utilize investigation and assessment (key items of basic intuition) thanks to take care of the given state of affairs or issue.

Obviously, every activity would require varied aptitudes and encounters, therefore make sure you scan the set of operating responsibilities cautiously and focus on the talents recorded by the business.

Top Critical Thinking Skills

Examination

Some portion of basic reasoning is the capacity to deliberately look at something, regardless of whether it is an issue, a lot of information, or a book. Individuals with

scientific aptitudes can analyze data, comprehend what it implies, and appropriately disclose to others the ramifications of that data.

- Posing Thoughtful Inquiries.

- Information Analysis.

- Research.

- Elucidation.

- Judgment.

- Addressing Evidence.

- Perceiving Patterns.

- Distrust.

Correspondence

Regularly, you should impart your decisions to your bosses or with a gathering of associates. You should have the option to speak with others to share your thoughts viably. You may likewise need to draw in basic deduction in a gathering. For this situation, you should work with others and impart viably to make sense of answers for complex issues.

- Undivided attention.

- Appraisal.

- Coordinated effort.

- Clarification.

- Relational.

- Introduction.

- Cooperation.

- Verbal Communication.

- Composed Communication

Inventiveness

Basic reasoning frequently includes imagination and development. You may need to spot designs in the data you are taking a gander at or concoct an answer that nobody else has thought of previously. The entirety of this includes an inventive eye that can adopt an alternate strategy from every different methodologies.

- Adaptability.

- Conceptualization.

- Interest.

- Creative mind.

- Drawing Connections.

- Inducing.

- Foreseeing.

- Incorporating.

- Vision.

Liberality

To think fundamentally, you should have the option to set aside any suppositions or decisions and only dissect the data you get. You should be objective, assessing thoughts without predisposition.

- Assorted variety.

- Reasonableness.

- Lowliness.

- Comprehensive.

- Objectivity.

- Perception.

- Reflection

Ways to Think More Critically

Presently we go to the part that I'm certain you've all been hanging tight for: how the hell improve at basic reasoning? Underneath, you'll discover seven different ways to begin.

1. Pose Basic Inquiries

Once in a while a clarification turns out to be unpredictable to the point that the first question get lost. To keep away from this, ceaselessly return to the essential inquiries you posed to when you set out to take care of the issue. Here are a couple of key essential inquiry you can pose to when moving toward any issue:

- What do you definitely know?

- How would you realize that?

- What are you attempting to demonstrate, negate, illustrated, study, and so on.

- What are you disregarding?

Probably the most amazing answers for issues are bewildering not due to their unpredictability, but since of their exquisite straightforwardness. Look for the straightforward arrangement first.

2. Question Basic Assumptions

The higher than discourse correspondence stays consistent once you're completely pondering a difficulty. It's completely straightforward to form Associate in nursing ass of yourself primarily by fail to research your essential assumptions. Likely the most effective pioneers in humanity's history were the people UN agency simply researched for a second and considered whether or not one amongst everyone's general doubts wasn't right., tending to doubts is that the spot progression happens.

You ought not to be unnatural to be a cheerful Einstein to learn by work your assumptions. That outing you have got needed to take? That recreation action you have got needed to endeavor? That section level position you have got needed to get? That attractive individual in your World Civilizations classification you have got needed to speak with?

All of these things are a reality within the occasion merely that you just} primarily question your assumptions and primarily measure your feelings with reference to what's affordable, fitting, or attainable. On the off chance that you just are looking for some help with this strategy, around then confirm the standing of Oblique methods. It's Associate in nursing instrument that performing artist Brian Enno and trained worker Peter national pioneer created to assist originative imperative reasoning. a small indefinite quantity little bit of the "cards" zone unit specific to music, all things thought-about most work for at no matter purpose you're stuck on a difficulty.

3. Understand Your Mental Processes

Human plan is astounding, nonetheless the speed and mechanization with that it happens will be a damage once we're making an attempt to suppose essentially. Our minds ordinarily North American nation heuristics (mental straightforward routes) to clarify what is going on on around us. This was valuable to folks once we were chasing monumental game and heading off wild creatures, but it o.k. could also be heartrending once we're making an attempt to decide on UN agency to choose in favor of.

A basic scholar is aware of concerning their psychological inclinations and individual partialities and the way they impact apparently "objective" selections and arrangements. We all have predispositions in our reasoning. Obtaining aware of them is that the factor that produces basic reasoning conceivable.

4. Have a go at Reversing Things

An extraordinary method to get "unstuck" on a difficult issue is to have a go at turning around things. It might appear glaringly evident that X causes Y, however imagine a scenario in which Y caused X.

The "chicken and egg issue" an exemplary case of this. From the start, it appears glaringly evident that the chicken needed to start things out. The chicken lays the egg, all things considered. Yet, at that point you rapidly understand that the chicken needed to originate from some place, and since chickens originate from eggs, the egg more likely than not start things out. Or on the other hand did it.Regardless of whether things being what they are, the turnaround isn't valid, thinking of it as can show you the way to finding an answer.

5. Assess the Existing Evidence

At the point when you're attempting to take care of an issue, it's constantly useful to take a gander at other work that has been done in a similar region. There's no motivation to
begin tackling an issue without any preparation when somebody has laid the foundation.

It's significant, be that as it may, to assess this data basically, or else you can without much of a stretch arrive at an inappropriate resolution. Pose the accompanying inquiries of any proof you experience:

- Who assembled this proof?

- How could they assemble it?

- Why?

Take, for instance, an examination demonstrating the medical advantages of a sugary grain. On paper, the investigation sounds truly persuading. That is, until you discover that a sugary oat organization financed it.You can't consequently accept this negates the examination's outcomes, however you ought to surely address them when an irreconcilable circumstance is so evident.

6. Make sure to think for yourself

Try not to get so impeded in research and perusing that you neglect to think for yourself–now and again this can be your most amazing asset. Expounding on Einstein's paper "On the Electrodynamics of Moving Bodies" (the paper that contained the celebrated condition E=mc2), C.P. Under the hundred "Maybein Einstein" range Goth Safgord was the Wolf under the standard of earnest money, freelance, his not -so-Movement in his Check-out. To an amazingly colossal degree, that is actually what he had done.

Try not to be arrogant, yet perceive that deduction for yourself is fundamental to responding to extreme inquiries. I see this as evident when composing papers it's so natural to lose all sense of direction in others' work that I neglect to have my own considerations. Try not to commit this error.

Critical Thinking

CHAPTER 3

Standard of essential thinking

Swim (1995) recognizes 8 attributes of number one reasoning. Truthful reasoning includes flow inquiries, characterizing associate degree hassle, analyzing proof, examining suspicions and dispositions, keeping a strategic distance from enthusiastic speculative, evading distortion, difficult over distinctive translations, and enduring unclearness. Dealing with ambiguity is similarly discovered by way of mistreatment as a basic piece of primary reasoning, "Vagueness and uncertainty serve an easy reasoning ability and location unit a essential and even a worth piece of the system"

Any other function of essential hypothesis regarded through numerous resources is metacognition. Metacognition is considering one's extraordinarily extraordinarily own reasoning. All the additional expressly, "metacognition is trailing one's instinct together performs express undertakings and in a completely whereas mistreatment this hobby to control what one is doing".

Important wondering, Beyer extravagantly clarifies what he sees as simple components of clean reasoning. these are:

Auras: important masterminds place unit distrustful, liberal, esteem honesty, regard evidence and thinking, regard lucidity and accuracy, take a goose at numerous views, and could change positions at the same time as cause drives them to try to to in and of itself.

Requirements: To expect essentially, ought to practice criteria.Must be compelled to have things that needs to be met for something to be created a name as achievable. Regardless of the fact that the opposition will be created that each branch of information has numerous standards, some of hints take a look at to all or any subjects. "Accomplice degree affirmation ought to be supported on relevant, specific actualities; in delicate of honest assets; actual; unbiased; liberated from clever mistakes; coherently reliable; and unquestionably pondered.

Rivalry: Is partner diploma statement or notion with assisting proof. Trustworthy reasoning includes characteristic, assessing, and building contentions.

Thinking: the electricity to surmise associate degree end from one or exceptional premises. to achieve this desires analyzing valid connections amongst proclamations or statistics.

Attitude: The method one perspectives the arena, that shapes one's improvement of importance. in a totally quest after experience, primary students see wonders from severa views.

Methods for growing use of requirements: unique forms of reasoning make use of a well-known contraption. Truthful reasoning utilizes severa strategies. Those techniques encompass move inquiries, developing selections, and function suppositions.

Lucidity

Questions that emphasis on clearness include:

• Could you expound on that point?

• Could you express that point in another manner?

• Could you give me a representation?

• Could you give me a model?

• Let me state in my very own words what I think you just said Tell me in the event that I am clear about your importance

Lucidity is an entryway standard. In the event that an announcement is indistinct, we can't decide if it is exact or important indeed, we can't inform anything regarding it since we don't yet have the foggiest idea what is being said. For example, the inquiry "What ought to be possible concerning the coaching framework in the united states?" is vague. To sufficiently address the inquiry, we would require a more clear comprehension of what the individual posing the inquiry is thinking about the "issue" to be. A more clear question may be; "What would educators be able to do to guarantee that understudies gain proficiency with the aptitudes and capacities that assist them with working effectively at work and in their day by day basic leadership?"

Lucidity is a significant standard of basic idea. Lucidity of correspondence is one part of this.We must be clear by the way we impart our musings, convictions, and purposes behind those convictions. Cautious regard for language is basic here. For instance, when we talk about profound quality, one individual may have at the top of the priority list the regular ethical quality of a specific network, while another might be thinking about certain transcultural principles of ethical quality. Characterizing our terms can enormously help us in the journey for lucidity. Unwavering focus is significant too; this implies we unmistakably comprehend what we accept, and why we trust it.

Exactness

Questions concentrating on making thinking increasingly precise include:

• Is that truly evident?

• How might we be able to verify whether that is precise?

• How might we be able to see whether that is valid?

An announcement might be clear however not exact, as in, "Many mutts gauge in excess of 300 pounds." To be precise is to speak to something as per the manner in which it really is People regularly present or portray things or occasions in a manner that isn't as per the manner in which things really are. Individuals much of the time distort or dishonestly depict things, particularly when they have a personal stake in the description_ Advertisers regularly do this to prevent a purchaser from seeing the shortcomings in an item. On the off chance that a commercial expresses, Our water is 100% unadulterated" when, in prevailing fashion, the water contains follow measures of synthetic concoctions, for example, chlorine and lead, it is mistaken. In the event that a notice says, this bread contains 100% entire wheat" when the entire wheat has been dyed and advanced and the bread contains numerous added substances, the notice is inaccurate.

Great masterminds listen cautiously to proclamations and, when there is explanation behind doubt, question whether what they hear is valid and precise similarly, they question the degree to which what they read is right, when declared as certainty. Basic reasoning, at that point, infers a sound suspicion about open portrayals concerning what is and isn't actuality.

Simultaneously, on the grounds that we will in general think from a limited, self-serving point of view, evaluating thoughts for precision can be troublesome. We normally will in general accept that our contemplations are naturally exact in light of the fact that they are our own, and in this manner that the contemplations of the individuals who can't help contradicting us are incorrect. We likewise neglect to address explanations that others make that adjust to what we as of now accept, while we will in general question articulations that contention with our perspectives. Be that as it may, as basic scholars, we constrain ourselves to precisely evaluate our own perspectives just as those of others. We do this regardless of whether it implies confronting inadequacies in our reasoning.

Exactness includes taking a stab at getting the issue viable before our psyches with a certain goal in mind. One approach to do this is to pose the accompanying inquiries: What is the issue at issue? What are the potential answers? What are the qualities and shortcomings of each answer?

Precision

Questions concentrating on making thinking female horse exact include:

• Could you give me more subtleties?

• Could you be progressively explicit?

An announcement can be both clear and precise however not exact, as in "Jack is overweight" (We don't have a clue how overweight Jack is - 1 pound or 500 pounds.) To be exact is to give the subtleties required for somebody to see precisely what is implied. A few circumstances don't call for detail. On the off likelihood that you simply raise, "Is there any milk within the fridge?' Further, I respond 'definitely' to each request and thus the unit of the appropriate reaction area is apparently substantially realistic (though it is important to take care of some milk, however). Or then again envision that you are sick and go to the specialist. He wouldn't state, "Take 1.4876946 anti-microbial pills two times a day." This degree of spectcity, or accuracy, would be past that which is helpful in the circumstance. Much of the time, be that as it may, particulars are fundamental to great reasoning. Suppose that your companion is having money related issues and asks you, "What should I do about my circumstance?" In this case, you may want to test its hypothesis for points of interest. Without the full points of interest, you couldn't support her. You may pose inquiries, for example, "What accurately is the issue? What precisely are the factors that bear on the issue? What are some potential answers for the issue in detail?

Precision is obviously basic to basic reasoning. So as to get at or closer to reality, basic masterminds look for exact and satisfactory data. They need the realities, since they need the correct data before they can push ahead and dissect it.

Importance

Importance implies that the data and thoughts talked about must be legitimately applicable to the issue being examined. Numerous intellectuals and government officials are extraordinary at diverting us away from this.

Importance is an announcement might be the entirety of the abovementioned however not huge. This is somewhat not the same as pertinence. You may locate that different components are important yet just a couple are noteworthy. For example, lung malignancy may have numerous causes (which are all important) however smoking is presumably the reason that is generally critical.

The entirety of this may appear "organized presence of mind" and in a way it is. Be that as it may, it's helpful to survey these norms periodically to recall how they fit together. I additionally prefer to audit the inquiries every once in a while so they're on the tip of my tongue when I get into a contention.

Like any ability or set of aptitudes, improving at basic reasoning requires practice. Anybody needing to develop around there may thoroughly consider these measures and apply them to an article in the paper or on the web, a blog entry, or even their very own convictions. Doing so can be a valuable and regularly significant exercise.

Consistency

Consistency is a key part of basic reasoning. Our convictions ought to be predictable. We shouldn't hold convictions that are conflicting. In the event that we find that we do hold conflicting convictions, at that point either of those convictions are bogus. For instance, I would probably negate myself on the off chance that I accepted both that "Bigotry is constantly indecent" and "Ethical quality is totally relative". This is coherent irregularity. There is another type of irregularity, called down to earth irregularity, which includes saying you trust a certain something, however doing another. For instance, in the event that I state that I accept my family is a higher priority than my work, however I will in general penance their inclinations for my work, at that point I am by and large for all intents and purposes conflicting.

The last 3 benchmarks are legitimate rightness, fulfillment, and decency. Consistent accuracy implies that one is taking part in right thinking from what we put stock in an offered case to the ends that pursue from those convictions. Culmination implies that we take part in profound and exhaustive reasoning and assessment, maintaining a strategic distance from shallow and shallow idea and analysis. Reasonableness includes looking to be liberal, fair, and liberated from inclinations and previously established inclinations that mutilate our reasoning.

Pertinence

Pertinence an announcement can be clear, exact, and exact however not pertinent. I once disclosed to my manager exactly how hard I was taking a shot at a specific undertaking. Her reaction was,

"So what?" It truly wasn't important.

Profundity

Profundity an announcement can be clear, exact, exact and significant yet shallow. Here's one: "On the off chance that we just wiped out sex ed in secondary schools, adolescents wouldn't get pregnant." Well, perhaps … yet by one way or another high schooler pregnancy is by all accounts an a lot further, increasingly convoluted issue. Key inquiry: Is that actually the most noteworthy factor?

Expansiveness

Expansiveness is an announcement can be clear, exact, exact, applicable and profound yet excessively restricted. Lawmakers do this consistently, exhibiting just the preservationist or just the liberal perspective. Simultaneously, we might be tight in our very own reasoning. So we may need to expand our own speculation just as "their" suspecting. Key inquiries: What about the opposite side? Consider the possibility that we flip the inquiry around.

Rationale

Rationale is an announcement might be the entirety of the abovementioned yet not coherent – it simply doesn't bode well. The coin hurl test demonstrates that analysis is more viable than acclaim is a genuine model. Key inquiries: How does that end stream from the proof? Are different variables included?

CHAPTER 4

The most effective method to
Learn Critical Thinking

A few perusers may think you must be keen to think fundamentally. In any case, a conclusion is that figuring out how to think basically makes you shrewd. T he supposition that will be that one can figure out how to think fundamentally (that is, be savvy). The supposition that is right. Here, I would like to give you how you can get more astute by learning basic reasoning aptitudes.

Expect Yourself to Think Critically

At the point when you read or tuning in to others talk, constrain yourself to turn out to be increasingly mindful and drawn in with the data. Posing inquiries guarantees commitment.

Learn and Look for Common Thinking Errors

Lamentably, most grown-ups are not shown formal rationale, even in school. School rationale courses are electives and are made befuddling by harsh premises, suggestions, and conditions. In any case, presence of mind rationale can do the trick. I have posted a rundown of normal reasoning blunders elsewhere.[1] Here are a portion of the more genuine reasoning mistakes:

Bid to power or accord: endeavoring to legitimize the end by citing an expert in its help or based on what number of individuals hold a similar view.

Contextual selection: Ignoring the specifics (regularly known as "filtering out"). Contradictory positions should be included in order to be satisfied. Ordinarily, contradicting contentions, in any event, when wrong by and large, as a rule have some trace of validity that should be suited.

Round thinking: thinking where the reason of a contention or an end is utilized as help for the contention. For the most part, this happens when proof is missing or bypassed.

Psychological easy route inclination: resolutely staying with a favored view or contention for a position, when other progressively productive potential outcomes exist. Indeed, even chess experts, for instance, may utilize a set up gambit when a superior strategy is accessible.

Mistaking relationship for causation: attesting that when two things happen together, and particularly when one happens just before the other, that one thing causes the other. Without other more straightforward proof of causation, this supposition that isn't supported. The two occasions could be brought about by something different. Model: downpour and lightning go together, yet neither causes the other.

Selectiveness disarray: inability to perceive components of similarity in various obviously clashing thoughts or realities. It is critical to know whether they are autonomous, good, or fundamentally unrelated. Model: ideas of advancement and creationism, as they are commonly utilized, are fundamentally unrelated. Be that as it may, expressed in different ways, they have shared components of understanding.

Falso similarity: clarifying a thought with a relationship that isn't parallel, as in looking at apples and oranges. While analogies and allegories are ground-breaking explanatory devices, they are not comparable to what they reference.

Forming a hasty opinion: utilizing just a couple of certainties for a complete end. The most well-known circumstance is inability to think about other options. A related reason is inability to address and test suspicions used to land at an end.

Learn Specific Strategies

Know about your reasoning. Disclose to understudies the need to consider how they think. This is the craft of thoughtfulness, concentrated on monitoring such things as one's very own level of readiness, mindfulness, inclination, passionate state, investigation of translation alternatives, confidence.

Train the capacity to center. In the present performing various tasks world, understudies normally come up short on the capacity to think. They are effectively diverted. They don't listen well, and are not powerful at separating significance from what they read.

Use proof based thinking. Try not to mistake supposition for truth. At the point when others make a case, don't acknowledge it without supporting proof. And, after its all said and done, search for opposite proof that is overlooked.

Distinguish what is absent. In discussion or perusing, the most significant focuses might be what isn't expressed. This is particularly evident when somebody is attempting to convince you of their perspective.

Pose inquiries and give your own answer. I had an educator, C. S. Bachofer at Notre Dame who constructed an entire course dependent on this guideline. For each understanding task, he required the understudies to pose a provocative inquiry about the perusing and afterward compose how it may be replied. Individual understudies discussed each other's inquiries and answers. Building up this as a reasoning propensity will guarantee you will end up being a progressively basic scholar, find out additional, and give some level of edification to others with whom you communicate.

Step by step instructions to Improve Critical Thinking

Having the option to think basically is a fundamental ability. You have to swim through what everybody is stating and select reality from the babble.

Basic reasoning isn't only for recognizing counterfeit news, be that as it may. You additionally need it to settle on precise choices. Would it be a good idea for you to purchase a house or lease? Eat paleo or vegan? Head off to college or drop out and start an organization? Every one of these choices is troublesome and significant, so having the option to ponder them can have an enormous effect in your life.

All things considered, what's the most ideal approach to improve your capacity to think basically?

The Wrong Way to Improve Critical Thinking

I'm going to begin with what I accept is the incorrect method to improve basic reasoning, which is tragically the caring regularly instructed in schools.This methodology begins by showing you some fundamental standards of consistent reasoning, modus ponens, a few instances of false notions and an entire bundle of Latin phrasing that logicians use. You work through a couple of issue sets and, voila!, you should have the option to reason basically about certifiable issues.

While there's nothing amiss with contemplating rationale and levelheadedness, as such, I don't think these strategies convey on their planned guarantee. Specifically, there's a couple of realities about how our mind really reasons that make this course to improved reasonability a questionable one.

Issue #1: Critical Thinking isn't a Faculty

The principal issue was really settled over a hundred years back by clinicians Edward Thorndike and Robert Woodworth. The mainstream perspective on learning of their day was the possibility that human cerebrums contained huge, unmistakable "resources, for example, rationale, memory and judgment, and that by rehearsing them on subjects, paying little mind to their significance to this present reality, would reinforce these resources simply like lifting loads in the exercise center improves your muscles.

The issue is that this hypothesis of the psyche doesn't work. The mind isn't care for a muscle. Rather than general, dynamic resources that can be improved with vague preparing, enhancements to the mind will in general be incredibly explicit. General enhancements, when they occur, will in general outcome out of the aggregation of many, numerous particular upgrades, as opposed to disconnected and general ones.

Think about learning a language. The workforce see says that learning Latin will improve your semantic resources. While there's some advantage of this, the greater part of crafted by learning a language is learning explicit jargon. Along these lines, on the off chance that you need to learn Japanese, you're best off learning Japanese jargon—acing Latin initially won't support excessively.

Essentially, basic reasoning isn't only a solitary solid capacity that diminishes to extract intelligent structures. Rather it's various actualities, deductions, heuristics and setting explicit capacities that must be developed through voluminous introduction to genuine circumstances.

Issue #2: Reasoning is Largely Rationalization

The contentious hypothesis of reason, which I shrouded inside and out here, recommends that the appearing disappointment of numerous sorts of human explanation are misconstrued in light of the fact that they don't perceive reason's actual capacity.

Rather than a universally useful method for settling on better choices, reason is a workforce for creating clarifications and assessing those of others. The insight originates from all through the cerebrum, by means of generally natural modules which are explicit and prepared through training, instead of some magical staff that does basic reasoning.

On the off chance that this hypothesis is right, at that point another explanation basic reasoning is difficult to improve is that we're for the most part not concocting increasingly wise choices when we think basically, however attempting to make all the more engaging contentions for our positions (or progressively sharp assaults on the contentions of others).

While this type of basic thinking through discussion has extraordinary advantages for our aggregate information, independently it doesn't support to such an extent. Rather, basic reasoning when utilized alone will in general be all the more a device for supporting your instincts instead of systematically assessing them to settle on better choices.

The Right Way to Improve Critical Thinking

So if the great perspective on basic reasoning isn't right, what's the correct method for doing it.

- I believe there's two wide approaches that will work to settle on better choices:

- The first is making a setting that will prompt better choices, considering what we think about human thinking as of now.

- The second is to assimilate parts and heaps of information about the world and coordinate it through work on deciding—as it were, basic suspecting originates from being savvy.

Technique #1: Creating Contexts that Enable Smart Decisions

This first technique is to perceive what you're really doing when you're thinking about things and utilizations this information to attempt to abstain from committing normal errors. Given what we think about how reason functions, there's a couple of things you can do:

1. Inspect the choice in numerous occasions, spots and mind-sets.

Since reason will in general be more to legitimize than to produce the correct judgment, one approach to abstain from committing errors is to reason about a similar issue in a variety of settings.

The measured hypothesis of mind says that instead of a solitary composed capacity, the cerebrum comprises of a great deal of semi-independent modules that all "vote" their favored activity into the cerebrum. Contingent upon which module is all the more unequivocally enacted by the setting around you, its vote will get higher weight. So in case you're ravenous, frightened, irate, tired, cheerful or pitiful you may get various contributions to which choice is right.

In this way, thinking about a choice in different states of mind, spots and settings will give you the best assortment of backgrounds to reason about things. In the event that the choice is the equivalent each time, you're can be increasingly certain that you have the right evaluation.

2. Converse with more individuals and have more discussions.

The contentious hypothesis of reason recommends that reason doesn't work very well alone. Be that as it may, it works splendidly when joined out in the open discussion. Some notable issues of human thinking vanish once you get a gathering of individuals together and let them talk about it.

Talking about your choice or judgment with others is a decent method to see your thoughts invalidated or let more grounded thoughts win the day. Despite the fact that there's a danger of gathering think and congruity pressures, in the event that you take an enormous and assorted enough gathering, you're bound to be presented to the best thinking, which will in general prevail upon the larger part feeling.

3. Try not to stake your notoriety on your decision.

Perhaps the greatest test to defeat in basic reasoning is that you may not appropriately refresh your convictions despite new proof. Old convictions may stick tenaciously to their earlier position, even once you're demonstrated to not be right.

Some portion of this might be on the grounds that, in a pugnacious hypothesis of reason, we are attempting to legitimize our natural convictions as opposed to contend against them. In this way, in case you're searching for why you're correct, you normally disregard why you're off-base.

Nonetheless, another huge part may be the social results of flip-slumping on your position. On the off chance that your notoriety and personality is staked on a thought

being correct, you very likely won't refresh adequately when you're uncovered with reasons that undermine your perspectives.

I've attempted to counter this inclination in myself by expounding on when I'm off-base. By sharing these reversals of convictions, I'm wanting to isolate myself from the substance of my thoughts, with the goal that I can dispose of the ones that don't work, as opposed to stick to them because of a paranoid fear of looking silly.

Technique #2: Be Smarter and Know More

The second way to deal with improving basic reasoning which really works is to just study the world. The more you think about things, the better you can reason about them.

I as of late had an encounter of this when somebody disclosed to me that they were concerned the wifi signals from their telephone may cause malignancy.

I clarified this doesn't bode well. Wifi signals are microwave radiation (and exceptionally low power). Disease is caused when DNA is harmed. For that to occur, radiation should be sufficiently vivacious to break sub-atomic bonds. Bright radiation is sufficiently able to do this (which is the reason you should put on sunscreen), yet unmistakable light isn't (which is the reason you needn't bother with sunscreen inside). Microwave radiation is an even lower recurrence than that, so it can't cause malignant growth.

The issue wasn't that this individual didn't have great basic reasoning abilities. It's not absurd to accept another innovation may have unstudied outcomes (counting causing malignancy). In the event that you heard this from a companion who you believe is really shrewd about different things,that is not a horrendous method to settle on a choice about the hazard.

The issue rather was that this individual didn't think enough about electromagnetism to perceive any reason why this case didn't bode well. On the off chance that they did, they ought to be a whole lot progressively stressed over every one of the lights yielding higher-recurrence obvious light at higher power each day than the black out light emission put out by the telephone.

Basic reasoning, along these lines, doesn't occur on the grounds that you've examined some theoretical consistent structure and come to substantial conclusions. It happens in light of the fact that you think enough about how the world attempts to preclude certain conceivable outcomes as being improbable or unthinkable.

The drawback to this is it implies basic reasoning can't simply be gotten by taking a couple of credits in school. It implies you should adapt always, pretty much all subjects, so as to settle on keen choices.

The upside is that it additionally implies a lot more astute choices are conceivable. A long way from simply being a theoretical workforce you either have or you don't, basic reasoning is a piece of the way toward realizing things in any case, and that you can improve at it by adapting more for an incredible duration.

Critical Thinking

CPSIA information can be obtained
at www.ICGtesting.com
Printed in the USA
LVHW081923010621
689024LV00017B/1610